More of...
Layton Looks
at
Life

by

William W. Layton
A Virginia Octogenarian

Published by
William W. Layton

© 2001
ISBN 0-9649806-0-6
Library of Congress Control Number:
2001116804

Typesetting by
The Piccadilly Printing Company
Winchester, Virginia

Printed by
Kirby Lithographic Company
Arlington, Virginia

Table of Contents

The Answer: "Not Today"

Introduction

Preface

Essays

Great Minds, Great People

The Answer: "Not Today"
(with *Addendum)

You ask me what my life is like today?

I cannot take the time to tell you now

Because I cannot stop to analyze

Each moment with its urgent whats and whys

Or how I meet and greet and how I touch

Each person that I pass along the way.

Perhaps tomorrow I can take the time

To tell you what I said and did today

And how it touched my soul and shaped my mind.

My friend, that's all I am prepared to say.

*Addendum

Remember please, my friend,

"Tomorrow is another day."

So raise your questions with me then,

For only God knows now what I will say.

William W. Layton
Washington, DC

Introduction

It was with a great deal of reluctance and many reservations that I agreed to pen this brief introduction to my father's book. In our family, it is not the custom to openly express one's emotions and affections. We're not a demonstrative clan, by any stretch of the imagination. Yet, nothing short of baring my soul, in this most public and permanent of fora, will suffice to express my regard for this most wonderful, intelligent, compassionate, and charismatic man, my father, William Wendell Layton. So, I'll give it a go.

I have the best father that anyone, anywhere, any time, could have, of this I am sure. Every positive trait, characteristic, strength-of-character, and all of my accomplishments, both personal and professional, I can clearly trace back to one or both of my parents. I can see it all in them, in the way they live their lives, treat others, and view the world around them.

From my father I gained the following, and this is by no means an all-inclusive listing: love of God; love of the printed word; a thirst of knowledge; love of my country, and a keen interest in its history, both glorious and shameful; love of people of every hue and from every walk of life; a strong sense of civic responsibility; true family values, with not a hint of the mean-spirited or judgmental about them; the ability to forgive; the ability to experience joy in the smallest of things – the trill of a bird, the color of a flower, the tiniest trinket, a poem, and a song; and, above all, eyes that look out on the world with hope, optimism, curiosity, and abiding faith.

I remember my father singing to the radio when he arose on cold, dark Michigan winter mornings, I remember the day he brought a puppy home in a box, and the day he brought home "Old Shep," the record that reduced me to tears, and "La Traviata" and "Porgy and Bess," and especially "The Importance of Being Earnest," and how he laughed uproariously each time we played it. I remember cozy weekend afternoons with the Sunday New York Times and Harpers and Atlantic Monthly, and how he revelled in our canasta games and trips to the tennis courts (I was an awful player) and the beach, how we played Hoop-X in the sand (I was an awful player), and Sunday drives after church, and the jewelry-making kit and the Frank Buck "Bring 'Em Back Alive" movies and the cartoons he showed us on a bedsheet hung up on the wall, and the "Night Playgrounds" he held in our Columbus, Ohio backyard, for us and all the neighborhood kids, where we stayed up past dark and played games and pulled strings to see which prize we would draw from a wash tub. I remember how proud he was of my reading and that he never censored my early literary pursuits, I remember his library and my first, tentative attempts at reading "adult" books, with his colletions of short stories of Maugham and Zola and de Maupassant that forever changed me, and how I never looked back, never returned to the Bobbsey Twins or Nancy Drew.

We may have come of age in the American Midwest, in the Ohio and Michigan of the 1940s and 1950s, but my father brought the world home to us and we embraced it all. We were of African descent, in a time when that conveyed a status in this land akin to that of the Untouchables of India, and not only in the South, but my father rose above this, and he carried us with him. He taught us to love our race, yet to not hate others, to not despair, to protest indignities and ill treatment, and to treat all people as we would want to be treated.

He taught me that I was the equal of every person, but not their better. And I felt safe and secure growing up in a sometimes hostile world, because my father was always there, and I believed that he could do anything – and he could.

In healthier times, he could work with his hands and make beautiful cabinets, use the most complicated Leica camera, beat almost anyone at tennis, compose poetry, deliver spell-binding speeches, hang wallpaper, clean a kitchen floor better than anyone else (down on his hands and knees with a razor blade to first remove the scuff marks), and drive us safely across nearly half of this country to Viriginia every summer, singing and joking and teasing and teaching all the way. I knew he could move mountains, and nothing could harm us.

A sense of security and of self-worth are among the greatest gifts a parent can give a child. My greatest hope is that I have passed some measure of these gifts on to my own children. If so, then I have done my father proud.

My father is still the most interesting and engaging person I know. He still fills every place he occupies with music and laughter and learning. You never know what he will bring you next – a poem, a Civil War document, a slave bill, a tiny trinket, the song of a bird, but always he brings joy.

Andrée Layton Roaf
Justice, Arkansas Supreme Court, 1995-1996
Judge, Arkansas Court of Appeals, 1997 - present

Preface

There are three reasons why we have chosen to publish this second book of essays in which we ruminate on subjects as disparate as the **antics of flying fish** to the **preciousness of lasting friendships.**

Reason Number One: An experience I had early in the morning of July 17, 1999, my 84th birthday, when I was jolted by the first news I heard when I turned on my bedroom TV. It was a report on the loss at sea of John F. Kennedy, Jr.'s airplane – John F. Kennedy, Jr., the 36-year-old son of President John F. Kennedy, Sr., killed by an assassin's bullet at the age of 48 years. What jolted me was that at 84, I had equaled numerically, in years, the combined ages of father and son Kennedy. It was simple arithmetic, 48 + 36 = 84. Later that day, at a gala birthday party given me by my daughter Mary and Nigel Parkinson, I kept turning over in my mind that poignant reality, 48 and 36 equal 84! I asked myself, "Was it Divine Will or was it the capriciousness of fate?". My answer was not long in coming. It came to me out of my Judeo-Christian tradition and belief. It <u>was</u> **Divine Will! Also, it was then that I was able to put the matter to rest as I concluded that there are vital lessons to be learned from the human tragedies we experience here on Earth.** Some of those lessons are delineated in the pages that follow in this book.

Reason Number Two: The inspiring words of appreciation I received in a letter from Sgt. Maj. Ric Van Norton USMC (ret.).

> *In your 80+ years you have made a difference in the world around you. Your influence is sound, ethical, positive and constructive. You have touched one more soul in your contact*

with me. I will forever look at you as one of my mentors. I hope I never disappoint you. Thanks for the great book. It ought to be required reading for __all__ Americans.

Thanks again for your kindness to me --- perhaps I can repay you in some small way by using a lesson from your book to repay a kindness to some other unsuspecting soul I meet along the road of life.

Reason Number Three (the predominant reason): The love and friendship of my family and friends -- especially my dear friend John Morrison -- who have said to me "keep writing. We think you have something to say that needs to be said." My motivation to publish this book was engendered by a loyal and enduring friendship with John.

Most of the essays in this book, with

some minor changes, first appeared on the cover pages of my service club monthly newsletter, **The Clarke County Kiwanian,** for the period 1996-2000. It is my hope that you will enjoy it as much as those who said they enjoyed my first book of essays. Nothing would please "OLD Bill" Layton more.

William W. Layton
Millwood, Virginia
February 2001

Great Minds,
Great People

"It's in the Book – #1"

Several years ago I wrote an essay in which I said that Mark Twain and Satchel Paige were two of my favorite personalities. Well, now I am sharing with you a piece from Letters from the Earth: The Uncensored Writing of Mark Twain, about which Twain said: "This book never will be published because it would be a felony." Well, it was published; I have it, and here is a piece from it entitled "At the Funeral":

- Do not criticize the person in whose honor the entertainment is given.
- Make no remark about the equipment (the casket). If the han-

dles are plated, it is best to seem not to observe it.

• If the odor of the flowers is too oppressive for your comfort, remember that they were not brought there for you, and the person for whom they were bought suffers no inconvenience from their presence.

• Listen with as intense an expression as you can command to the official statement of character and history of the person in whose honor the entertainment is given; and if these statistics should seem to fail to tally with the facts, in places, do not nudge your neighbor or press your foot upon his toes, or manifest by any other sign, your awareness that taffy is being distributed.

• At the moving passages, be moved – but only according to the degree or your intimacy with the parties giving the entertainment, or with the party in whose honor the entertainment is being given. Where a blood relation sobs, an intimate friend should choke up, a distant acquaintance should sigh, a stranger should merely fumble sympathetically with his handkerchief. Where the occasion is military, the emotions should be graded according to rank, the highest officer present taking precedence in emotional violence, and the rest modifying their feelings according to their position in the military service.

• Do not bring your dog.

"It's In The Book – #2"

We had so much fun with the essay by Mark Twain from his book <u>Letters from the Earth</u> that I decided to do another from that same book. Well, here goes:

This offering is on the proper behavior of a young man in a fire in a boarding house (for you youngsters, the old term for an "apartment building"). Twain said "the true gentlemen will always save the young ladies first-- making no distinction in favor of personal attractions, or social eminence, or pecuniary predominance -- but taking them as they come, firing out with as much celerity as shall be consistent with decorum." There follows a rescue-order-of-priority list of 27, with the first 12 as follows:

1. Fiancées. 2. Persons toward whom the rescuer feels a tender sentiment, but has

not declared himself. 3. Sisters 4. Step-sisters 5.Nieces 6. First cousins 7. Cripples 8. Second cousins 9. Invalids 10. Young lady relations by marriage 11. Third cousins and young lady friends of family 12. Unclassified.

Twain then says that numbers 1, 3, 4, and 5 may be "carried from the burning house in the rescuer's arms – permission being first asked, and granted; numbers 7 and 9 may be carried out without permission; the others may not be carried out, except they themselves take the initiative, and signify, by word or manner, their desire to be rescued, in order of priority are: 13. Babies 14. Young widows 18. Elderly widows 19. Clergymen 23. Landlady 26. Furniture. Guess who is 27, the last on the list of those to be rescued. The answer probably got Twain in "a barrel of trouble," for #27 is Mothers-in-law!!!! I better run for cover for having the audacity to write this piece. Goodbye till next time. I hope.

"An Unforgettable Day!"

On April 12, 1945, I was in Piqua, Ohio, attending a civil rights conference sponsored by the Ohio Congress of Industrial Organizations (CIO). That was 10 years before the merger of the CIO with the American Federation of Labor (AFL). During a break in the meeting, two other conferees and I were standing on the front steps of the building in which the conference was being held having a "cigarette break" when an elderly man passing the building yelled at us. He said "YOUR president is dead." Almost in unison the three of us said "What president?," to which he replied in a hostile tone, reflecting a strong political bias, "YOUR President Franklin D. Roosevelt." We immediately returned to the meeting and reported what we had heard and a radio was turned on confirming the report of the old man. Amid the sobbing and cries of "What will we do now with Roosevelt gone," the conference adjourned. For months, yes, even to this day, the shock of the news of April 12, 1945 is felt by many people.

British Prime Minister Winston Churchill made the following statement concerning Roosevelt's death.

> It may be said that Roosevelt died at the supreme climax of the war, and at the moment when his authority was most needed to guide the policy of the United States. When I received these tidings early in the morning of Friday, the 13th, I felt as if I had been struck a physical blow. My relations with this shining personality had played so large a part in the long, terrible years we had worked together. Now they come

to an end, and I was overpowered by a sense of deep and irreparable loss....

In a message to Mrs. Roosevelt he said:

Accept my profound sympathy in your grievous loss which is also the loss of the British nation and of the cause of freedom in every land. I feel so deeply for you all. As for myself, I have lost a dear and cherished friendship which was forged in the fire of war. I trust you may find consolation in the magnitude of his work and the glory of his name.

Every April 12th I will close my eyes and I know I will again hear the old man's words, "**Your** president is dead."

"Ballard Trent Edwards: Virginia Statesman"

My maternal great-grandfather, Ballard Trent Edwards, was one of the most inspirational and influential leaders in Virginia's history. For eight years, he served as a member of the House of Delegates in the General Assembly, representing the counties of Chesterfield and Powhatan and the town of Manchester.

His grandfather, Edward Bradbury Edward, Sr., a large Chesterfield landowner, was recorded a freeman when he was born in 1763, so obviously his father must have been free also.

Ballard's father, Edward B. Edwards, Jr., was born in 1800, and in 1826 married Mary

Trent, a school teacher, also free, and a county landowner. As a youth, Ballard was exposed to an intellectual environment rare among children of his racial group.

When the U. S. Civil War ended, thousands of slaves faced freedom not equipped for its responsibilities, largely unskilled and unschooled. Ballard Edwards was now ready to extend his helping hands to those to whom in days past he could only show his silent compassion.

With his wife, Sarah Ann Coy, a Pamunkey Indian born in 1833, whom he married in 1850, Edwards opened, at his expense, a school to teach hundreds of former slaves to read and write and the useful and economically productive trade of bricklaying.

Upon Virginia's re-admission into the Union, Edwards was the unanimous choice of the Republican Party to be candidate to represent their district in the state legislature. He easily won without serious opposition.

In 1870, the gallery of the old House of Delegates Chamber collapsed. It killed 63 people and injured several hundred others. A hue and cry went up throughout the State of Virginia to tear down the venerable building and "replace it with a temple of state suitable to the esteem of this great Commonwealth." Such a bill was introduced into the General Assembly. With his knowledge of sound construction, Edwards made an impassioned speech, begging the legislators to rehabilitate the landmark. He pointed out how the building could be remodeled and restored to a safe and attractive condition for far less than the cost of a new building. He also reminded them of the building's sacred connection with Washington, Henry, Madison, Jefferson, Monroe and other heroes of the nation's past. His plea helped sway the balance of votes and the General Assembly opted for renovation, thereby saving one of the nation's greatest landmarks.

Edwards' second important legislative victory was his crusade for a free bridge across the James River, as the only bridge at that time was the Mayo Bridge, a toll bridge that had been used since the late 18th century. Thus, on June 6, 1873, the Ninth Street Bridge was opened for the free use of all Virginians. It remained in use until 1973, a hundred years later, being replaced by the Manchester Bridge.

After three terms, Edwards, in 1877, did not seek re-election, and was succeeded by another black, his protégé, Henry Cox. Edwards devoted the rest of his life to his extensive church work and the training of young blacks in the construction trades. Also, before his death in 1881, he served several terms as Justice of the Peace in the Town of Manchester and as Overseer of the Poor for the County of Chesterfield.

This essay was based on a biographical sketch of Edwards by Robert W. Waitt, Jr.

Bill Layton visits the Pamunkey Indian Museum in King William County, Virginia.

"MARCHing Along With Bell"

I recently acquired a marvelous electronic device that has brought me a feeling of security that I would not have thought possible just a few years ago. Oh, I suppose I could say I am fairly sophisticated when it comes to radio and television theory, and yes, even to the functions of the dreaded personal computer (dreaded by most folks in my age bracket). You see, I am an old "Ham" (the term given to licensed amateur radio operators), starting back in 1925, when I constructed a little $1.50 crystal radio receiver into which I plugged a pair of headphones. And boy, oh boy, what a thrill I got when I heard the announcement: "This is Radio Station WRVA, Richmond, Virginia, down where the South begins."

But now, let's talk about our little "new miracle." It is a cellular telephone. Wow, what a great little marvel it is. It has a call-waiting signal, an answering machine, a phone book from which I can automatically dial designated phone numbers, clock, a calculator, and three or four other features I haven't had the time or the courage to explore. Now, "old Bill Layton" feels like he has the world at his right-hand-index-finger's reach!! Any minute now, I might buzz your number.

This being the month of March, I thought I ought to say a word or two about the inventor of the telephone who was born on March the 3rd, 1847 - - Alexander Graham Bell.

Many others had long tried to transmit the human voice before Bell, and many have helped improve and perfect Bell's invention. But Bell will always be known as the father of the electric telephone. Born in Scotland, educated at the universities of Edinburgh and London, Bell moved to Canada in 1870. His main interest throughout his life was in helping the deaf and in 1871 he started teaching deaf pupils. In 1872 he began teaching at Boston University and in 1877 married 18-year-old Mabel Hubbard, one of his pupils who had been deaf from early childhood.

In Boston, on March 10, 1876, the first sentence was successfully transmitted by telephone. They were the historic words to Bell's assistant: "Mr. Watson, come here, I want you." Bell's remarkable invention was featured at the Centennial Exposition in Philadelphia in 1876. Six years later Bell became a citizen of the United States.

Among Bell's other inventions was an audiometer for measuring the intensity of sound. He also experimented in aviation and in 1898 became President of the National Geographic Society. Alexander Graham Bell died on August 2, 1922. During his funeral service, every telephone of the Bell System was kept silent.

"Timeless Words"

Many years ago, I wrote an essay on the life and work of Dr. George Washington Carver, whom I consider to be one of the truly great personalities of all time. With so much being reported in the electronic and print media on the discord and violence throughout the world, I thought it might be helpful to speak again about the "great botanist benefactor". The following is taken from a little booklet on Carver written by Glenn Clark. Mr. Clark introduced Dr. Carver at a religious convention in Minneapolis in 1939, the year, incidentally, that I visited with Dr. Carver in his research laboratory in Tuskeegee Institute in Alabama.

Dr. Carver rose and walked slowly toward the front of the plat-

form. *"I am disappointed in the intro-duction Professor Clark made of me. I don't think he did a very good job. I always look forward to introductions about me as good opportunities to learn a lot about myself that I never knew before."* Instantly the audience burst into happy laughter and from that moment it was completely in his hands. Dr. Carver now, to our dismay, walked away from the loud speaker to the left of the rostrum and began his address. But to our amazement and joy his voice was loud and clear -- with a silver, musical quality in it which carried to the farthest corners of the huge auditorium. I never heard a voice with greater carrying power. It was as though he utilized unused hidden vibrations, in the ether, not used by the average speaker.

"Years ago," he continued, "I went into my laboratory and said "Dear Mr. Creator, please tell me what the universe was made for?"

"The great Creator an-swered, "You want to know too much for that little mind of yours. Ask for something more your size."

"Then I asked, "Dear Mr. Creator, tell me what man was made for." Again the great Creator replied, "Little man, you are still asking too much. Cut down the extent of your request and improve the intent."

"So then I asked, "Please Mr. Creator, will you tell me why the peanut was made?"

"That's better, but even then it's infinite. What do you want to know about the peanut?"

"Mr. Creator, can I make milk out of the peanut?"

"What kind of milk do you want, good Jersey milk or just plain boarding house milk?"

"Good Jersey milk."

"Then the Creator taught me how to take the peanut apart and put it back together again. And out of this process have come forth all these products." For over an hour Dr. Carver drew forth from his homemade box of samples a continuing procession of face powder, printer's ink, butter, shampoo, creosote, vinegar, dandruff cure, instant coffee, dyes, rubberoid compound, soaps, salads, wood stains.

"The great Creator gave us three kingdoms, the animal, the vegetable, and the mineral. Now he has added a fourth, the synthetic king-

dom." And as he proceeded with his lecture I breathed to myself, "and the greatest of all seems to be the synthetic kingdom."

Dr. Carver in the lab.

"Fateful Days"

Every year I think of where I was when the assassination of two of this nation's foremost personalities occurred – President John F. Kennedy and the Rev. Dr. Martin Luther King, Jr. At the moment that President Kennedy passed, I was on a Northwest Airlines flight from Cleveland, Ohio to Lansing, Michigan and when the plane landed in Detroit, enroute, the dire news was announced by a member of that airport's ground crew. The word of Dr. King's death I heard from a passerby as I left a Pep Boy's store in Northwest Washington, DC, where I had gone to purchase some batteries for a portable radio. I was stunned, rendered speechless, and cannot remember, to this day, how I made my way to my car. But the enormity of the situation was brought to me as I heard the sounds of the many police and fire truck sirens, for portions of Northwest DC were literally in flames.

In the spring of 1968, Dr. King was organizing a march of the poor -- black and white -- on Washington to "dramatize the whole economic problem of the poor..." "We need an Economic Bill of Rights so as to guarantee a job to all who want to work and are able to work and guarantee an income for all who are not able to work." He went to Memphis, Tennessee, interrupting his work for the Poor People's March, to support the strike of 1,300 black sanitation workers.

On April 4, 1968, Dr. King was assassinated as he stood on the balcony of a motel in Memphis. The night before, he told an audience that he had "seen the promised land" of victory in his fight for equality and justice, but "I may not get there with you." Oh how prophetic were those words! He ended that speech with these words:

"Our world is a neighborhood. We must all learn to live together as brothers or we will all perish as fools. There are two challenges to America. The challenges are racism and poverty. In a few weeks, a few of us are coming to Washington to see if the will to meet these challenges still lives among us. We are going to bring those who have known long years of hurt and neglect. We are not coming to engage in any historic action. We are not coming to tear up Washington. We are coming to engage in dramatic, non-violent action. We are coming, and we will stay as long as we have to… We will suffer and die if we have to. For I submit, nothing will be done until people put their bodies and souls into this."

Less than 24 hours later, Dr. King was dead.

DRAWING OF DR. KING
BY DON MILLER

"Paul Robeson and the Here and Now"

1998 marked the 100th anniversary of the birth of Paul Robeson, truly a "one of a kind" American. The son of a runaway slave who became a minister, Robeson was valedictorian of his Rutgers University class of 1919, where he won 15 varsity letters in four sports and was named an "All American" football great twice. A graduate of the Columbia University Law School, Robeson was admitted to the bar. But his law career was very short, with other career paths proving more interesting to him. His career as an actor started in 1920 and led to a Broadway debut the following year. Among his many stage successes are: The Emperor Jones, The Hairy Ape, and Othello. He began singing professionally in the late 1920's, and in the 1930's and 1940's was the world's leading concert singer. He starred in American and British films, but voluntarily ended his film career in 1939. The rest of his life was dedicated to music and the theater, and to what I consider his greatest contribution to the world: his fight against racism and for world peace. Because of his work for world peace and recognition given him by governments throughout the world, including the Soviet Union, he was accused of being a Communist and his United States passport revoked. He moved to England in 1958 and continued to give concerts in Europe and the Soviet Union, returning to live in the United States in 1963 until his death in 1976. William Pickens, III is president of the Paul Robeson Foundation, Inc., established in 1996 to preserve and extend Robeson's rich legacy of humanism, civil rights activism and excellence in scholarship, athletics, and the performing arts. I can think of no more timely emphasis in this critical point in our nation's history than that mission.

In 1978 (80th anniversary of Robeson's birth) I was asked by a religious organization to write a poem honoring Robeson's memory. The following are the last two verses of that poem, "A Paul Robeson Retrospective":

> What would he have us do to
>   honor him,
>
> We who now strive to cleanse a
>   nation's sin?
>
> What is the price of absolu-
>   tion now
>
> For what we were and what we
>   might have been?
>
> I hear that great voice as it sings
>   and speaks,
>
> The tone, pitch, volume, resonant
>   and clear.

It says to us fight on, the task is
ours;

The time is always now; the place
is here.

"Valuable Words"

Literary scholars, as well as others the world over, have long proclaimed Lincoln's Gettysburg Address as one of the truly great works of prose in the English language. But few know of the difficult circumstances under which it was written or the condition of Mr. Lincoln's health at the time he delivered it.

According to records related to the Gettysburg ceremonies, President Lincoln did not receive the invitation to speak from the chairman of the committee to create a national cemetery at the battlefield until two weeks before the event. The principal speaker, the famous orator Edward Everett, was invited two months before the event, which took place on November 19, 1863. Added to the short time to prepare, it is reported that Mr. Lincoln, at the time, was suffering from what was described as a "mild case of smallpox".

Lincoln wrote one page of his speech in Washington on White House stationery on November 17 and added the final lines in his bedroom in Gettysburg the night of November 18. The following morning (the day of the event) he wrote a new draft, making a few changes. The final draft consisted of only 269 words. Everett's address lasted two hours

> *"Fourscore and seven years ago our fathers brought forth on this continent a new nation, conceived in liberty and dedicated to the proposition that all men are created equal."*

while Lincoln's speech was just under three minutes. An analysis shows that Lincoln used five words with one letter ("a"), forty-six had two letters, forty-four had five, twenty-five had six, thirty had seven, and the rest eight or more. There were only eighteen words of three or more syllables.

> *"The world will little note nor long remember what we say here, but it can never forget what they did here."*

Many in the audience of 15,000 expressed great disappointment at Lincoln's performance and most newspapers ignored his participation in the event or had negative criticisms. However, the next day Everett wrote Lincoln a letter in which he expressed his admiration for Lincoln's words, adding, "I would be glad if I could flatter myself that I came as near the central idea of the occasion in two hours, as you did in two minutes." The first real positive applause came from the

Chicago Tribune, which said that the speech would "live in the anals of man." And, indeed it will! Just conside this: of the five known copies penned by Lincoln, autograph experts report three have been sold commercially at an average rate of about $2,225 a word. This is known to be the highest price brought by written words!

"...from these honored dead we take increased devotion to that cause for which they gave the last full measure of devotion -- that we here highly resolve that these dead shall not have died in vain, that this nation under God shall have a new birth of freedom, and that government of the people, by the people, for the people shall not perish from the earth."

"The TRUTH about Sojourner"

One of the most delightful experiences for me this summer has been reading about the exploits of the little electronic robot probing the far-off planet of Mars. My interest has been heightened because the marvelous little 25-pound, six-wheeled vehicle is named "Sojourner" in honor of Sojourner Truth, the Black freedom fighter and champion of women's rights who lived during the Civil War era. She was born a slave in 1797 (?) in upstate New York and died in Battle Creek, Michigan in 1883.

Truth's legal name was Isabella Van Wagener, but she changed it to Sojourner Truth because, she said, "The Lord named me 'Sojourner' because I am to travel up and down the land showing the people their sins and being a sign unto them."

> *"It is only logical that the Pathfinder be named Sojourner Truth because she (the robot) is on a journey to find the truth about Mars."*

The National Aeronautics and Space Administration (NASA) selected the name "Sojourner" from an essay in a contest to name the robot. The winning name was in an essay submitted by a 12-year-old black, Bridgeport, Connecticut girl, Valerie Ambroise, who wrote, "I chose Sojourner because she was a hero to Blacks, slaves and women. She acted on her strong feelings about life and the way it should be. Her greatest companions were God and her beliefs." She added, "It is only logical that the Pathfinder be named Sojourner Truth because she (the robot) is on a journey to find the truth about Mars."

The contest judges picked Ambroise's paper from more than 3,500 submitted by students worldwide.

And now, "Sojourner", thanks for giving us some much-needed thrills in a summer when too often the headlines have been on death and destruction visited upon us by nature and by that class of creatures known as homo sapiens!

Cheers and keep cool.

"Harriet Tubman – Part I"

Harriet Tubman was the "Moses of her people", truly one of this nation's greatest heroes. Born a slave in 1821 on the eastern shore of Maryland, by the time she was six years old, she had absorbed many kinds of knowledge. She could not have said how or at what moment she learned that she was a slave. Around the same time someone had also taught her where to look for the North Star, the star that stayed constant, not rising in the east and setting in the west, and told her that anyone walking toward the North could use that star as a guide. She also knew moments of pride as when the overseer consulted Ben, her father, about the weather. Ben could tell if it was going to rain, when the first frost would come, and whether there was going to be a long stretch of clear sunny days.

As a teenager she sought and found jobs that would keep her outdoors. She learned most of the woods-lore from her father: the names of birds, which berries were good to eat and which were poisonous, and where to look for plants to cure all sorts of ailments, fevers, and intestinal disorders.

Harriet's father taught her to pick a path through the woods, even through the underbrush, without making a sound. Neither of them ever discussed the reasons why it was desirable to be able to go through the woods soundlessly. Discussion wasn't necessary. Deep inside herself Harriet knew what Ben was doing. He was, in his own fashion, training her for the day when she might become a runaway, and successful flight would depend on the skill of her movements through the woods that bordered all the roads. When she was 19, he rewarded her efforts with praise. She had followed him through the woods and though he moved quietly himself, he had not heard her, although she was close behind him. When they reached a clearing, she came up in back of him and touched him lightly on the arm. He jumped, startled, and then laughed when he saw Harriet standing beside him.

Thus was Harriet Tubman's training by her father that equipped her to become the most celebrated "Underground Railroad Conductor" in United States history.

"Harriet Tubman – Part II"

In the last essay we told of Harriet Tubman's training by her father for the work that would earn for her the sobriquet "Moses of her people." Thus at an early age she knew that the Underground Railroad was not a railroad at all. Neither did it run underground; it was composed of a loosely organized group of people who offered food and shelter, or a place of concealment to fugitives who had set out on a long road to the North and freedom. In 1849 she set out on the journey that led to her own freedom, finally arriving in Pennsylvania after having traveled 90 miles from Dorchester County, Maryland. She had slept on the ground at night. She had been rowed up the Choptank River by a man she had never seen before. She had been hidden in the attic of the home of a Quaker. When she crossed the line into the free state of Pennsylvania, she said, "I looked at my hands to see if I was the same person now that I was free. There was such a glory over everything, the sun came like gold through the trees, and over the fields, and I felt like I was in heaven." But when she thought of her family, left behind in Maryland, all of them slaves, she decided that as soon as she could she would go back to Dorchester County and lead them North, too.

From 1851 to 1857, the country moved closer to civil war. During these years Harriet Tubman made 11 trips into Maryland, bringing out members of her family and other slaves.

After the death of John Brown in 1859, Harriet began to feel dissatisfied with the life she was leading. She had become famous for her work, but the many audiences before whom she spoke offered no challenge to her ingenuity or her imagination. She longed to return to Maryland to bring out more slaves.

It was John Andrew, the Governor of Massachusetts, who was responsible for Harriet's final major role. During the Civil War she became a scout, a spy, and a nurse for the Union forces.

In many ways Harriet Tubman represented the end of an era, the most dramatic, the most tragic era in American history. She died on March 10, 1913. Of all her great work, Harriet Tubman will be remembered always as a conductor on the Underground Railroad escorting bands of trembling, frightened slaves out of Tidewater area of Maryland to an unimagined free life to the North.

On July 12, 1914, the city of Auburn, New York, her last home location, paid tribute to her; flags were flown at half-mast and a bronze tablet was placed on the front entrance of the courthouse. It reads:

IN MEMORY OF
HARRIET TUBMAN
BORN A SLAVE IN
MARYLAND ABOUT 1821
DIED IN AUBURN, N.Y.,
MARCH 10TH, 1913
CALLED THE MOSES OF
HER PEOPLE,
DURING THE CIVIL WAR,
WITH RARE COURAGE SHE
LED OVER THREE HUNDRED
SLAVES TO FREEDOM,
AND RENDERED INVALUABLE
SERVICE AS NURSE AND SPY.
WITH IMPLICIT TRUST IN GOD
SHE BRAVED EVERY DANGER
AND OVERCAME EVERY
OBSTACLE. WITHAL SHE
POSSESSED EXTRAORDINARY
FORESIGHT AND JUDGMENT SO
THAT SHE TRUTHFULLY SAID
"ON MY UNDERGROUND
RAILROAD I NEBBER RUN MY
TRAIN OFF DE TRACK AN' I
NEBBER LOS' A PASSENGER."
THIS TABLET IS ERECTED BY
THE CITIZENS OF AUBURN.

"A Fateful October Night"

On the night of October 16, 1859, an event took place that was to forever shape the course of our nation's history. For it was on that night that the Federal arsenal at Harpers Ferry, Virginia, was attacked by the ardent abolitionist John Brown and his raiding party. During the months before the Civil War, and even today, many people look on John Brown as a martyr to the cause of abolishing slavery. Others regard him as an insane criminal. However, today most historians generally regard him as a man of great conviction who chose a lawless course in his efforts to achieve a good end.

Brown, born May 9, 1800, in Tarrington, Connecticut, was one of a family of 16 children. At 15 he was doing a man's work and followed many trades in his lifetime, including farming, tanning and surveying. He married at 20 and fathered seven children. A year after the death of his wife in 1823, he married a second time, a union that produced 13 children.

Like his father, Brown was a staunch abolitionist and believed that slavery was a sin. When his family moved to Pennsylvania, his home was a station on the Underground Railroad and he had many contacts with Harriet Tubman.

When the Kansas question was settled in favor of freedom, Brown drew up a scheme for eradicating slavery in the South. On a rented farm in Hagerstown, Maryland, he gathered a few men, including several blacks, and attacked the Harpers Ferry arsenal. He wanted to seize the arsenal and induce slaves to escape. He captured the town, but was besieged by local authorities and the United States Marines under the command of

Colonel Robert E. Lee. Most of Brown's men were killed or taken prisoner, but a few escaped. Two of the slain were Brown's own sons, and he himself was wounded and captured.

Brown was tried and convicted by the state of Virginia of treason, murder, and inciting slaves to rebellion. He was hanged at Charles Town, Virginia (now West Virginia) on December 2, 1859. At his trial he declared he would "forfeit my life for the furtherance of the ends of justice, and mingle my blood further with the blood of my children and with the blood of millions in this slave country whose rights are disregarded by wicked, cruel, and unjust enactments…"

Withing 18 months from that fateful night of October 16, 1859, this nation's Civil War had begun, a war of brother against brother that ultimately cost over 600,000 lives.

"Lee, Lincoln, and a Lot of Bull"

In September 1862, General Robert E. Lee began withdrawing his troops from Sharpsburg, Maryland, following the Battle of Antietam. That being the case, we decided to bring you a favorite Lincoln story involving a bull, for your edification as well as your enjoyment. So here goes the Lincoln yarn:

Some supporters of the Union cause were opposed to any accommodation or yield to the South because they felt that since the South started the war, it should be held responsible to the last stage for whatever came in the future. Lincoln said that reminded him of a vicious bull in a pasture that took out after everybody who tried to cross the lot. One day a neighbor of the owner was the victim.

This bull, being at a disadvantage and not able to either catch the man or extricate his tail, was mad enough to eat nails. He dug into the earth with his feet and bellowed so you could hear him two miles or more and at length broke into a dead run, the man hanging onto his tail all the time.

While the bull, much out of temper, was legging it to the best of his ability, the man still clinging to the tail asked, 'Darn you, who started this fuss?'

Lincoln concluded his bull story by saying "It's our duty to settle this Civil War at the earliest possible moment, no matter who started it. That's my idea of it."

"Lincoln's Fateful Second Inauguration"

Unlike our winter of 1997-98, so far, the winter of 1864-65 had been extremely cold, with ice so thick on the Potomac River that it could easily support crowds of people skating on the river. But Inauguration Day, March 4, broke in a torrent of rain. The city was packed with visitors come to witness the event. Many who had been unable to find accommodations actually invaded the Capitol Building and slept there while Congress itself stayed awake all night to finish its final business.

In mid-morning the rain slackened slightly and crowds began to gather on the grounds of the Capitol to attend this, the first inauguration to be held in front of the new iron dome and its recently erected statue of Freedom. About eleven o'clock the grand procession formed around the White House and Lafayette Square to march along Pennsylvania Avenue, unaware of the fact that Lincoln had already proceeded them and was busily signing last minute bills. The rain stopped, but the mud it had created flooded the streets (no paved streets in that day) so thickly that it was difficult to wade through. Yet the procession somehow reached the Capitol and, by the scheduled time of shortly after noon, the mud-spattered throng had swelled to an estimated total of 30,000.

Shortly before twelve, Andrew Johnson (the Vice President-elect) entered the Senate chamber to take the oath of office, but before doing so, delivered a long speech which provided nothing except that he was under the influence of liquor, and it delayed the whole proceedings. Then the dignitaries moved to the east front of the Capitol. An incident occurred which went unnoticed at the time, but a man tried to break through toward the President, he was later identified from a photograph as the actor John Wilkes Booth.

At about one o'clock the President rose, amid applause, and gave his address that included the memorable words:

> "With malice toward none; with charity for all; with firmness in the right as God gives us to see the right let us finish the work we are in...."

"Great Words from a Great Man"

For more years than I can recount I have been an ardent "Lincoln buff". As a youngster, I literally read everything I could find in the public and my school libraries, magazines, text books, etc. on our 16th President, Abraham Lincoln. One of the most thought-provoking items I read is a portion of a speech Mr. Lincoln gave on September 30, 1859, to the annual meeting of the Wisconsin State Agricultural Society. The following is that piece.

It is said an Eastern monarch once charged his wise men to invent him a sentence to be ever in his view, and which should be true and appropriate in all times. They presented him the words, "And this, too, shall pass away." And yet, let us hope, it is not quite true. Let us hope rather, that by the best cultivation of the physical world beneath and around us, and the intellectual and moral world within us, we shall secure an individual, social, and political prosperity and happiness, whose course will be onward and upward, and which while the earth endures, shall never pass away.

More cogent words were never, or will ever, be spoken!!!

"February – Tension and Tonic"

Each year, February is celebrated as Black History Month in hundreds of communities throughout the United States. In so doing, public and private schools, churches, civic groups, and other institutions and organizations recognize the role Black Americans have played in the building of our nation. For each of the past five years we have presented a serious narrative in February. This year, feeling that we ought to try to relieve the tension built up in many of us from the big doses of violence and politics being fed us in the news media, we would do a humorous piece -- an account of an actual incident that occurred in Rochester, New York in 1852. And one that involved no less a person than Frederick Douglass, the great abolitionist.

Douglass, known for his eloquence, forceful manner and brilliant logic, had just finished delivering his famous oration, **What to the Slave is the Fourth of July?** It is reported that as his voice rose in passion he thundered: "Your celebration is a sham; your boasted liberty an unholy license; your national greatness, swelling vanity...". Among those seated in the audience were the white minister and deacon of the local Rochester Baptist Church.

"That was a mighty fine speech for a Negro," commented the deacon.

"Not when you consider he's half white," said the minister.

"You don't say!", exclaimed the deacon. "Just think, if only half a Negro can speak that well, what could a whole one do?"

And now, with my apology for presuming that you need a **humorous verbal tonic**, I wish you a happy February Valentine's Day!!!

Fine Friends, Feathered and Unfeathered

"Has He Gone to THE DOGS?"

I have heard many, many great stories about dogs during my lifetime and for some unknown reason, perhaps buried deep in my psyche, I was inspired to write this piece on "the dog." **The DOG:** That animal reputed to be "man's best friend" and the subject of much prose and poetry, of whom Mark Twain once said: "If you pick up a starving dog and make him prosperous, he will not bite you. This is the principal difference between dog and man." There is no mistaking it, when it comes to fidelity, Twain picks dog over man!

(Let the sleeping DOG lie)

Anthropologists say the dog's ancestry can be traced back to a five-toed, weasel-like animal called Miacis, which lived in the

Eocene epoch about 40 million years ago. Miacis is the forebearer of the cat, racoon, bear, hyena, and civet, as well as of the wolf, fox, jackal, and dog.

After many intermediate stages covering millions of years, the Miacis moved into the genus Canis, which includes the dog, wolf, and jackal, all of which developed into their present forms about a million years ago.

Authorities agree that the dog was the first of man's domesticated animals. How and when this took place remains a mystery. A 50,000-year-old painting in a cave in Europe shows a dog-like animal hunting with man.

 One popular theory is that dogs were attracted to the food scraps dumped as waste near human sites. As the dogs kept the sites clean, humans in turn would accept their presence and not drive them

away. However, some dogs, such as the dingo of Australia, have returned to the wild state.

(Hair of the DOG)

In the middle ages many European hound breeds were developed by the nobility for "coursing," in which the hunted prey is pursued until exhausted and then killed. Coursing was eventually replaced by fox hunting as we practice it today, because it is considered less cruel than coursing.

(Every DOG has his day)

Man has been amply repaid for his long partnership and rapport with the dog. Care and love have been rewarded with loyalty, companionship and fun from his "best friend."

(It's raining DOGS and cats)

I close this piece with some doggone popular expressions:

• "I work like a **Dog**" every day, but I have a neighbor who is as "lazy as a **Dog**".

• When I go on a date I always "put on the **Dog**".

• When I owe people money they "**Dog** my footsteps".

• There are bird **Dogs**, watch **Dogs**, hot **Dogs**, and under**Dogs**.

And now, I'm **Doggone** tired of writing, so goodbye, **Doggone** it!

"And Now He Says:
LET THE CAT OUT!"

Many writers have extoled the virtues of "the dog," that four-leg creature whom many animal lovers have described as "man's best friend." Now while I appreciate that, I hasten to say that forced to choose between dog and cat, it's the cat for me every time. And I have some great company on my side in my animal preference -- folks like Mark Twain, who once said: "If man could be crossed with the cat, it would improve man, but the cat would deteriorate." Now tell me, was Twain speaking his true belief or was he engaging in his famous sardonic humor? What do you think?

Cat or dog, whichever one you prefer, they both originated according to anthropologists, from the same source, a weasel-like animal called the Miasis some 40 to 50 million years ago. But, the experts add that the cat apparently existed for millions of years before the first dogs appeared.

The first association of cats with humans may have begun toward the end of the Stone Age. Much later, about 5,000 years ago, cats were accepted as members of the households of Egypt. The Egyptians used the cat to hunt fish and birds as well as to destroy the rats and mice that infested the grain stocks along the Nile. Also, it was considered so valuable that laws protected it and eventually a cult of cat worship developed that lasted more than 2,000 years. Soon all cats became sacred to the Egyptians. After a cat's death, its body was mummified and buried in a special cemetery.

In Europe, during the Middle Ages, the cat became an object of superstition and was associated with evil, an associate of witches and perhaps the embodiment of the devil. Thousands of cats were hunted, tortured and sacrificed.

By the 17th century the cat had begun to regain its former place as a companion to people and a controller of rodents. Many writers began to keep cats as pets and to write of their good qualities. By the 1800's cat shows were being held in England and the United States, and cat-fancier organizations were established. However, many of the old superstitions are still evident today in the form of such sayings as "a black cat crossing your path brings bad luck".

There are "Felix the Cat," "Tom and Jerry," "Hodge," "Puss in Boots," and of course, in the Clinton White House, that much celebrated white-footed feline, "Socks." Boy, oh boy, cats sure have come a long way! And if my "cat sense" is accurate, I would say that they are even now scheming to go quite a ways more. Oops! See what I have just done in divulging what I think cats are up to. Yes, I have just "let the cat out of the bag".

"Birds of a Feather"

First it was the dog. Then it was the cat. Now we take "literary flight" on the subject of "the bird." But first, a question: What is a bird? The quick answer "off the top of one's head" is: "It's an animal that flies." But that answer would be wrong, for what about butterflies, which are insects, and bats, which are mammals? Some birds, on the other hand, do not fly at all. Take for example the ostrich, the emu and the kiwi, all of which can run very fast, or the penguin that swims. So you see, none of the above fly!

Of one thing you can be sure, all birds have feathers. So it is feathers, not flying, that make a bird a bird. Also, all birds are warm blooded with backbones and two legs. And whether they fly or not, all have wings, have a beak instead of a jaw, lay eggs, and most build a nest (some steal nests from other animals).

In researching the subject of birds for this essay, I became so fascinated with one species that I decided to share my newly-gained knowledge with you. It is about the **Secretary Bird**, the only bird that lives and hunts primarily on the ground and is best known as killer of snakes. Unlike the human office secretary, it does not have a boss!

A native of the uplands of Africa, the Secretary Bird is so named because the tuft of stiff feathers on the back of its head and neck makes it look like an old-time secretary with a bunch of quill pens stuck behind the ear. It is sometimes kept by farmers to kill snakes, rodents, reptiles, and large insects. It kills its prey by kicking, stomping, or flailing it against the ground. If its victim does not succumb, the bird may snatch the animal, take flight, and drop the victim from aloft. Tell me, how often wouldn't a human secretary like to accord to similar treatment to an inconsiderate caller at the office?

And now, in conclusion, a suggestion for the office secretary: Preserve this essay and when you ask for a pay raise, read it aloud to the boss and then say to him or her, "Now aren't you glad I'm not like the Secretary Bird?". Please let me know what happens.

"Finishing With THE FISH"

So far we have expounded at length on the dog and the cat, and to a lesser degree on other creatures, including, of course, the human animal. We thought, this time with the year soon to expire, we would "finish with the fish". But first, a question: What is a fish?

Any animal that lives in the water is usually called a fish. Perch, crawfish, cuttlefish, jellyfish, starfish, seals, and whales all live in water. Yet only the perch, in this list, is a true fish. Seals and whales are warm-blooded mammals. The others belong to the great group of animals "without backbones". A fish is a cold-blooded animal with a backbone. It lives in water and breathes by means of gills. It has two pairs of fins in place of arms and legs, as well as several other fins, and many are covered with scales.

Frogs, salamanders and toads who breathe under water by means of gills and have backbones are known as amphibians. How then can one tell a fish from an amphibian? The difference is in those two pairs of limbs. In the amphibians they are legs, in the world of fish they are fins. Fish never have legs!

Fish are fascinating in their variety, and we have chosen one that is especially fascinating for this essay's subject: the flying fish, for it can actually fly through the air for long distances. It takes to the air with two wing-like fins that are attached to either side of its body. They are really elastic membranes that, when spread, serve as "wings". The flying fish does not fly for pleasure, usually leaving the water only when it is pursued by its enemies, which are sharks, tuna, porpoises and dolphins. First, it increases its swimming speed, and when swimming fast enough, it swoops out of the water. It often attains a speed of 35 miles an hour. As it takes off it spreads its fins and soars out of its enemies' reach. The flying fish can stay aloft from two to 15 seconds and can span from 45 to 200 yards. Wow!

And now, in closing, some advice to my fine friends who fish: Armed with the above flying fish facts, when you return home after a poor catch or none, you can explain the situation with the words: "I had bad luck. The big one flew away!" Cheers.

Notable Times

"A Primary Fact of Life"

As a youngster (here comes some old fashion Layton nostalgia), I recall reciting the little ditty, "April showers bring May flowers." This month I thought I would edify you with the original Layton two-liner in the Human Procreation category: "May conceptions bring February births" – of course, nine months later, as if you didn't know that!

And what an array of talent February has brought forth! Just to name a few: Abraham Lincoln 2/12; Babe Ruth 2/6; Susan B. Anthony 2/15; Mary 1st of England – "Bloody Mary" 2/18 (now, I've got to get a shot of booze to continue writing this essay after mentioning "Bloody Mary"); George Washington 2/22; Henry W. Longfellow 2/27; and please don't forget the famous "Harlemof-the-1930's" poet Langston Hughes, born February 1, 1902!

Want some more? Here goes.
February:

3 - Horace Greeley, Gertrude Stein

4 - Charles Lindbergh

7 - Charles Dickens

10 - William T. Tilden

19 - George Peabody

20 - Mary Garden

21 - Cardinal John Henry Newman

23 - George Frederick Handel

28 - Linus Pauling

29 - Rossini

And now, March, come on with your old bad winds so we can get ready for sweet April and warm, seductive **May!**

"A Halloween Lesson (Males Take Note)"

In 1997, because of illness, I missed two October events that I annually look forward to with great anticipation. I left Millwood, Virginia via an ambulance the morning of September 23, 1997, spent two days in the Winchester Medical Center and an additional day in the Washington Hospital Center. I had what is termed a TIA episode (fancy acronym for a mini stroke). I did not return to my "Downtown Millwood" residence, except for a day or two, until July of 1998. But enough about my misfortunes.

The October events I refer to are, one, the annual reenactment of the October 19, 1864 Battle of Cedar Creek, held a short distance south of Middletown on U.S. Route 11 (Valley Turnpike) at the Belle Grove

Plantation, and two, Halloween, a time when I annually entertain on my front porch 45 to 50 youngsters from the Millwood, Boyce and Berryville area.

What I want to tell you about now is an experience I had Halloween night, 1996. The youngsters came to my front porch in groups of two to six or seven, enthralled by my gaily decorated front porch featuring lighted scarecrows, skeletons, etc. Among the handouts (candy, fruit, toys) that I gave each child in 1996 was a gold-colored band ring set with a bright-colored stone (red, blue, green or white-fake diamond). At one point, a group of three girls came to my porch, two about eight years old and the third child appeared to be three or four. With much gusto, I gave the two older girls what I described as "beautiful diamond rings." To the youngest I said "And to you I give a beautiful red ruby ring." Much to my surprise and chagrin, the tiny tot, with a deep frown on her face said, "Mr. Layton, I want a diamond ring, too!"

I could only conclude that Boy oh Boy, even at three or four years old a female knows that "Diamonds are a girl's best friend!" GENTLEMEN TAKE NOTE!

Bill Layton enjoys Halloween with neighbor-hood children in Millwood, Virginia.

"Christmas Over the Years"

What started out as a one-day celebration, as far back as 336 AD, has now become a "Commercial Bonanza": a lengthy holiday season embracing at least the whole month of December. In this country the Christmas season begins on Thanksgiving Day and ends on January 1st, New Year's Day -- a period of about five weeks. The reason for this extended holiday period is that Christmas is no longer only a religious festival, it is also the most popular holiday period where Christianity is the dominant religion. Even in Japan, as well as in many other countries where Christianity is the minority religion, Christmas has become a festive gift-giving holiday time.

Gift giving is one of the oldest customs associated with Christmas; it is actually older than the holiday itself and was started to compete with the ancient pagan festivals that occurred about the same time. As Germanic tribes of Europe accepted Christianity and began to celebrate Christmas, they also gave gifts. In this country the exchange of gifts has become so significant that most merchants count on making a large portion of their annual sales during the period from late November to December 24th. (Get out the credit cards, folks).

Trees and greenery, lights and fires also have a pre-Christian origin, as they were used by the Egyptians, Chinese, and Pre-Christian Europeans at the New Year to scare away demons. For Northern Europeans this winter celebration was the happiest time of the year because it signified that the shortest day of the year, about December 21st, had passed and that the days would start to get longer and brighter.

Of all the Christmas stories, none is better known or more popular than Charles Dickens' "A Christmas Carol". I read it as a youngster, and my guess is that you also read it when you were young. The best known character in the story is Ebenezer Scrooge, who has come to stand for his unloving, selfish, and miserly behavior, and the ending of the story, after Scrooge has mended his ways, presents a meaningful combination of the religious and non-religious nature of Christmas.

And now, A Happy and Spiritually rewarding Holiday Season to one and all.

Bill Layton in Millwood, Virginia, a winter wonderland at holiday time.

"February – Short on Days, Long on Heroes"

Every year when February comes around I reflect on the role that February plays in making our cal-endar turn out so precise in terms of how the seasons begin and end. It falls the lot of poor old February to  have only 28 days, with only one additional day every fourth year. Scientists say this is done to accommodate our solar year calendar, which is almost 11 days longer than a lunar year calendar that is 29 days, 12 hours, 44 min-utes and 2.8 seconds per month. But, so much for the scientific gobbleygook, let's just talk about February.

February has a special meaning for me, especially February 12 -- because my mother was born on that day in 1886 and, being a Civil War buff, my favorite American hero, Abraham Lincoln, was also born on that date in 1809. For as long as I can remember, I have celebrated those two birthdays in some special way. This year it will be a Lincoln Day banquet in the ballroom of the Officers' Club at Fort McNair in Washington, DC.

To honor our martyred President I give you a true story that few, if any, of you have heard.

Lincoln was born and reared among people who were believers in premonitions and supernatural appearances. He once declared to his friends that he was "from boyhood superstitious". Lincoln and his companion John Hanks visited an old fortune teller, a black voodoo woman. Tradition says that "during the interview she became very excited, and after various predictions, said: 'You will be president and all the slaves will be free.'" That the old voodoo woman should have foretold that the visitor would be president is incredible, but Lincoln, so it was reported, took it seriously.

"Giving and Getting"
Christmas 1997

One of the happiest, if not the happiest, periods of my life were the first twelve years. Certainly they were my most carefree years. I describe them thus because those years were spent in rural Hanover County, Virginia, less than two miles from the birthplace of Patrick Henry of "Give me liberty or give me death" fame. I am certain now, in my "old age", that much of my happiness as a youngster was due to the trees that abounded in the wooded area less than one hundred yards to the rear of the house in which we lived.

My brother, Ben, and I spent many hours with "our trees" and we gave each one of those trees a proper name. Our favorites were the large maples and oaks that we often climbed and there was one in which we built a platform that we called "our house". We ascribed human characteristics to the trees and talked to them, and believed that they listened to us and responded to our voices. You see, we truly loved those trees and we believed they loved us in return.

Our greatest thrill came each year when we, along with an adult with an axe, went into the woods in search of *the tree* that would grace the center of our living room from Christmas Eve through New Year's Day. Oh, how excited we became when we found that *one tree* that was chosen above all others for that place of honor in our home! It was always a large tree, at least six feet in height, and that rich, fir aroma emanating from it is still sharp to my olfactory sense after more than 70 years.

During my childhood most of the decorations for our Christmas tree were made at home. And what a joy it was to see the creative talent blossom in our Christmas "home workshops". Today the prime symbol of a modern Christmas is the brilliantly decorated artificial evergreen tree with strings of multicolored "store-bought lights".

Sadly, our Christmas celebrations have become so commercialized that their true meaning is lost to an emphasis on the gaily wrapped boxes under the tree. Wouldn't it be great if our celebrations this year would focus more on the _true meaning_ of Christmas and less on "what we give and what we get" in material things? How about giving it a try!

"Spring Has Sprung!"

As I was writing this essay (in mid-April) it occurred to me that I was daily sharing an experience with perhaps 95% of all the adult residents on the East Coast of the United States. And what is that common experience? I will give you three guesses. Okay, time's up. If you answered "Talking about the weather," you got the right answer. For since March 20th (the first day of spring), none of the conversations I have had has ended without some mention of the weather. "Oh, what a great spring day" or "Oh, what a lousy spring day." Then there are those "mixed-bag" days: bright, then cloudy, rainy, then clear. The combinations are variable if not exciting.

There is one thing certain about the weather. It does not play favorites; it treats alike rich and poor, saint and sinner. For virtually every living thing is affected by the seasons. People wear heavier or lighter clothing and eat different foods according to the weather. In most parts of the world they even play different games in each season. In my heyday it was tennis for me in the spring, summer, and fall. Now, as an "old man", it's the spectator "sport" of arm-chair watching my grandson William Layton Roaf, via TV, in his role as offensive tackle for the New Orleans Saints football team. I can work up a sweat sometimes just looking at the TV screen. Wow!

The seasons are still known by the names that dimly reveal primitive peoples' feelings about them. Winter is an old Germanic word meaning "time of water" -- of rain and snow. Spring refers to the springing forth of living things. The original meaning of summer and autumn are lost. We in the United States, however, generally call autumn by its alternative name, fall, from "fall of leaf".

Now, I want to close this essay on the subject with which it was begun: **Spring.** For I cannot end it without stressing the fact that spring is not all "sweetness and light," for it is a time of the year that we married men know as "Honey do" season. With house cleaning from attic to basement to be done, old papers and magazines to be gathered up and discarded, touch-up painting and minor repairs to be taken care of, the little "wifey-dear" comes into her own. "Honey do this" and "Honey do that" become the most popular words in the American wife's lexicon. Oh well, guys, just keep in mind that spring, like everything else, will pass. In a few months it will be fall again. And that means lounging in an easy-chair with a glass or can of our favorite beverage in one hand and the remote control in the other hand. We will really have it made then. Oh, how sweet it is!!

Building a Nation

"Proud Symbol of a Proud Nation"

When was the last time you had a guided tour of the U.S. Capitol? Or rather, I should ask, "Have you ever had a guided tour of our nation's capitol?" If it has been many years since you did, or you never have, now would be a great time to do so. I take the tour every four or five years and find it a great experience, as I always see something I had not seen on previous visits. To whet your appetite, I want to pass on to you a few facts on that great symbol of democracy, and I do so primarily in the words of my dear friend Mike Michaelson. Mike, a Richmond, Virginia native, came to the U.S. Congress in 1951 as assistant superintendent in the House Radio and TV Gallery, and became superintendent in 1974. In 1981, he became executive vice-president of C-Span. Mike is a great man and truly "one of a kind."

He has been leading tours of the Capitol for 40 years.

Times have certainly changed since the building was first constructed. In those early years, there was no air conditioning, no running water, no central heating, and no modern plumbing. Initially, privies and wells were located outside and fireplaces provided heat. Sunlight, whale oil lamps and chandeliers were the chief sources of light. Boats, which were anchored at the Capitol's West Front, were used for transportation in a canal that was later filled in to become what is now Constitution Avenue. There were also stables for members' horses and fences to keep out the cows that grazed on nearby farms.

Although other extensions and changes have been made over the years, the West Front center section is the last remaining original portion. For more than 100 years, presidential inaugurals were held on the East Front, but since Ronald Reagan's inauguration in 1981, the tradition has moved to the West Front.

The magnificent iron dome atop the Capitol weighs 8,909,200 pounds and is the largest and most beautiful in the world. The dome has 108 windows and 48 Corinthian columns. It was the first dome of its size to be made entirely of cast-iron. President Lincoln saw its completion as a symbol that the Nation would survive. The last section was put in place at exactly 12 noon, December 12, 1863. Unfortunately, Lincoln, who was confined to bed with a cold, did not attend the event.

"The New Nation – March 1790"

More than two hundred years ago, March 1, 1790, the U. S. Congress passed the Census Act, making this country the first nation to provide by law for a periodic census. The local record of that first census is on microfilm in the Handley Library in Winchester, and I have examined it. It is a fascinating record and you will find it an interesting experience to spend some time reviewing it. Also in March 1790, Thomas Jefferson became U. S. Secretary of State and Congress adopted the Naturalization Act, which set a two-year residency requirement for new immigrants.

Fears of British intentions with respect to the new nation persisted, and in early March 1790 it was rumored that the British would dispatch 10,000 soldiers to North America. There were also sporadic Indian raids which resulted in deaths of both whites and Indians, and in mid-March President George Washington publicly expressed concern for the safety of inhabitants of Western Virginia.

The question of slavery continued to be a very live issue, and a published letter from a free black citizen of Philadelphia declared that "Africans and Americans are all of one species." However, on March 23, 1790, a U. S. House of Representatives' committee reported that "Congress has no authority to interfere with slavery in the states."

Now, finally, a humorous note: On March 16, 1790, President Washington advertised a sale of "mares and jennets" at his home in Mount Vernon. To date, I have not seen (nor have I sought) any record of the results of what must have been an interesting sale by no less a person than the "father of our country."

"The Flag of the United States"

Very much in the news media is the continuing controversy over whether the First Amendment of our Constitution (the right of free speech) gives one the right of political expression by burning or otherwise mutilating the flag of the United States. A timely word on the history of the flag, to which we pledge our allegiance at every Kiwanis Club meeting, is therefore very much in order.

The United States Capitol Historical Society has published an unusually informative and attractive booklet on our nation's flag and the 50 state flags, seals, and mottoes.

The flag of the United States of America symbolizes the rich history and heritage of our nation. The 13 stripes, alternate red and white, represent the original 13 states.

The 50 stars on a blue background embody the 50 states that today comprise the United States.

The colors of the flag also embody the virtues on which the nation was founded. White is the traditional color of loyalty, while blue symbolizes unity, and red represents the sacrifice so often paid in blood that our nation might remain free. In 1777, the Continental Congress resolved that the flag of the 13 United States "be thirteen stripes, alternate red and white, that the union be thirteen stars, white in a blue field representing a new constellation." Since then, the flag has added stars as new states entered the Union. The last two were added in 1958 and 1959, when Alaska and Hawaii were admitted as states.

After Vermont and Kentucky were added to the Union, the flag was altered to 15 stars and 15 stripes in 1795. In 1818, President

James Madison signed a bill returning the number of stripes from 15 to 13, also providing for the addition of stars as new states were admitted.

"A Precious and Unexpected Gift to America"

I believe the great communication medium of television redeemed itself with five truly glorious evenings of authentic American history, the PBS series "The Civil War." As a result of what I saw and heard in that series, I know I can never be the same again, nor can I ever feel the same about my country and its people. Thanks to PBS, I forgive the television industry for all the ersatz offerings it has inflicted upon me and my household over the years. And, as for filmmaker Ken Burns, he is no less a hero than those heroes (Northern, Southern, well-known, unknown) who moved across my TV screen and into my heart, as alive today as they were in 1861.

As a collector of Civil War memorabilia for many years, I was deeply moved by a report that Ken Burns has carried a Civil War letter in his pocket for five years. It is a letter from a soldier to his wife in which he tells of his love for her and promises that if he does not return to her, the last breath that will escape him on the battlefield will whisper her name.

Many of the personal Civil War letters in my collection express similar feelings for family and friends as the letter Burns carries. But there are other and more mundane sentiments expressed as well. An example is a letter from a Yankee soldier to his sister dated September 14, 1864, written from "Camp near Berryville, VA."

In it he tells of the "very good times now days because we are encamped in rich country. We can get plenty of forage and fruits are very plentiful, such as apples and peaches. This is the greatest farming country in Virginia, but we are sweeping it clean."

Further on in the letter he reports: "One of our fellows asked an old farmer how he liked the Yanks. He said he used to like them, but he didn't any more for they was so bad that they took everything they had." The letter closes with an expression of the writer's love and the hope that he will soon hear from his sister as well as his mother.

Thus, just five days before the third and final battle of Winchester, the soldier, David Faust, sent a reassuring message home. Did he make it back to family and friends or did he fall at Winchester? Someday I will research the Civil War archives and find the answer to that question.

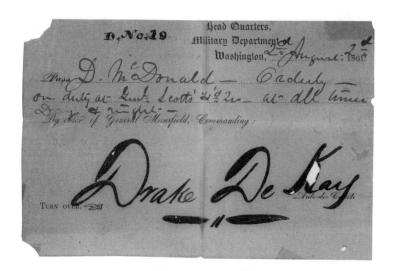

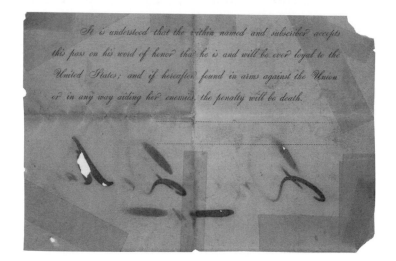

Civil War military pass.

"A Fateful July 21"

On July 21, 1861, one of the great battles of the 19th century took place. Known as the First Battle of Bull Run (Union designation) or First Manassas (Confederate designation), it was the first important land operation in the four-year military conflict that was to cost over 600,000 American lives and billions of dollars in physical property damage. It was described by a local resident, Cornelia McDonald, in the following words:

> The battle was called the battle of Bull Run, because it took place near that stream, a poor little mountain brook, that I remember playing in when a child, as my sister's home was near it. Near there was the great battle fought

that might have decided the issue if God had not willed that it should be decided not then or there. And now the homely name has become a classic, as much as any in ancient story, for as goodly men, and as glorious heroes dyed its waters that day with their blood, as any that ever fell on the hard-fought battlefield of the world.

It was thought by many persons, North as well as South, that the war would be of short duration, even possibly ending at Bull Run in a Union victory, because of the Union's superior military resources. Contemporary reports tell how congressmen, with their wives, daughters, and sweethearts, came out from Washington in luxurious carriages with baskets packed with champagne and food, to view from a safe distance, victory for the Union forces. Then, they thought, they would march on to Richmond. There was to be a great victory ball in Richmond and the ladies had provided themselves with magnificent dresses, expecting, after the battle they would view was over, to proceed to the Confederate capitol without opposition. Now, as just about everybody knows, it didn't happen that way. President Lincoln, learning of the decisive defeat of the Union forces, met with his cabinet to develop plans for what now seemed certain to be protracted struggle. Thus, six days after the Bull Run debacle, he handed over command of the Union forces to General George McClellan, replacing the badly defeated General Irvin McDowell.

"May 1861 - The Critical
First Days"

In a previous essay we discussed the actions of President Abraham Lincoln during the first 48 hours after the fall of Fort Sumpter, the military action which marked the beginning of the armed phase of the Civil War. This month we cover briefly some of the critical actions of both the Federal and Confederate governments in May 1861. These activities greatly influenced the character and outcome of the early battles, which for many months brought decisive Confederate victories.

The Northern Shenandoah Valley area figured prominently in the early actions, for on Wednesday, May 1, 1861, Confederate Major General Robert E. Lee, under authority of the Governor of Virginia, ordered volunteer troops located at Harpers Ferry under the command of Colonel Thomas J. Jackson (before the sobriquet "Stonewall") to move all machinery from the rifle factory there to Winchester and Strasburg. That same day Federal troops continued to pour into Washington and the Federal Navy placed a strict blockade at the mouth of the James River and Hampton Roads. Two days later Lincoln issued a call for 42,034 volunteers to serve for three years, unless sooner discharged, and Governor Letcher called for Confederate volunteers to defend Virginia.

On May 6, Arkansas and Tennessee left the Union and joined the Confederacy, the ninth and tenth states to take that action. On May 20, North Carolina, in convention, voted unanimously for secession, the eleventh and last full state to join the Confederate States of America. It should be noted that in Western Virginia the vote was overwhelmingly against secession, as it was already breaking away from the State. As a result, on May 23, 1863, Western Virginia organized a pro-Union government and was officially admitted to the Union on June 29, 1863 as the state of West Virginia.

Toward the end of the month (May 29) Confederate States President Jefferson Davis arrived in Richmond, the newly designated capital. It is reported great crowds hailed him as "Jeff Davis, the Old Hero".

Thus the die was cast; for four years (minus four days) we were a nation divided against itself. Some of the scars of the great tragedy remain to this day.

God Bless America!

"How Young is Too Young?"

While the U. S. Congress debates proposals regarding smoking and violence (yes, even homicide) by underage youths, we thought we would take a look at the underage youth participation (18 years and under) in the U. S. Civil War, sometimes referred to as "The Boy's War". Here are some figures:

- More than 2,000,000 Federal soldiers were 21 and under (of a total of 2,700,000)

- More than 1,000,000 were 18 and under

- About 800,000 were 17 and under

- About 200,000 were 16 and under

- About 100,000 were 15 and under

- 300 were 13 and under. Most of these were fifers and drummers, but regularly enrolled, and sometimes fighters.

- 25 were 10 and under

A study of a million enlistments turned up only 16,000 as old as 44, and only 46,000 of 25 or more years old. Confederate figures are not as fully reported, but one sample of 11,000 men produced about 8,000, the great majority between 18 and 21 years of age. There was one of 13 and three were 14; 31 were 15; 200 were 16; 366 were 17; about 1,000 were 18. Almost 1,800 were in their thirties, about 400 in their forties, and 86 were in their fifties. Robert E. Lee was one of the fifty-year-olds. One man was seventy and another was seventy-three.

Most of the youths of tender age slipped in as musicians, for there were places for 40,000 in the Union army alone. There are many stories of buglers too small to climb into saddles unaided, who rode into pistol-and-sabar battles with their regiments. Most famous of these on the Union side was Johnny Clem, who became drummer to the 22nd Michigan at eleven years and soon a mounted orderly on the staff of General George H. Thomas, with the "rank" of lance sargeant.

There was youthfulness in the General Officer category as well. Examples are: Philip Sheridan, USA, and John B. Hood, CSA, both generals at 30 years of age; J. E. B. Stuart, CSA, at 28 years; O. O. Howard, USA, Gouveneur K. Warren at 29; but topping the list are George A. Custer at 21 and the "top whopper", Brevet Major General Galusha Pennypacker, USA, at 17 and too young to vote until after the war's end.

As I wrote the last line of this essay at the age of 83 years and 17 days old, I said to myself, "Bill Layton, you are an old man, the adage of 'you are as old as you feel', to the contrary, not withstanding." Then I put my pen down for the day. See you next time -- same place.

"Wonders Never Cease"

As of this writing, there have been 30 days of the "air war" against Yugoslavia, with the question of whether there would be or should be a ground invasion of Kosovo. Further, there is the question as to what countries' troops would be employed should there be a "ground invasion". There is also increasing doubt that the "ethnic cleansing" of the ethnic Albanian population can be ended by air strikes of Yugoslavia alone, however massive they might be.

These questions have reminded me of the situation leading to -- in the first few days and weeks of our Civil War, which began on April 13, 1861 -- the surrender of Fort Sumpter. On Monday, April 15, President Lincoln issued a proclamation declaring that an "insurrection existed" and called out seventy-five thousand militia form the various Northern states. The response was immediate and overwhelming. Quotas were assigned to states and individuals were chosen by means of draft.

Many thousands of men did not want to go to war after being drafted, and hired substitutes to take their places. Among those to do so was a future president, Grover Cleveland. Even President Lincoln hired a substitute to take his place, although as president, he was not subject to the draft. A man by the name of John Staples accepted five hundred dollars to don a Union uniform to fight as Lincoln's substitute.

On the Confederate side, wealthy South Carolina plantation owner Wade Hampton, with no military training or experience, was eager to serve and formed military units at his own expense. After the war he was stripped of more than three thousand slaves.

Tennessee U. S. Senator Andrew Jackson was the only Southerner to remain in the U. S. Congress during the war and was chosen by President Lincoln to be his running mate when he (Lincoln) ran for his second and successful term for the presidency. Johnson succeeded to the presidency upon Lincoln's death in April 1865.

It is an astounding fact that Andrew Johnson was the only chief executive unable to write at the age of seventeen. He acquired that skill from sixteen-year-old Eliza McCardle whom he married in May 1827 WHEN HE WAS EIGHTEEN YEARS OLD. OH, MY, MY, MY.

"Fascinating Finds"

In my more than 50 years of collecting historical memorabilia (mostly U. S. Civil War documents and letters), I have had a number of "fascinating finds." Topping the list of those "finds" is a letter dated September 12, 1864.

This letter was sent to Lt. Colonel John Wooley in Baltimore from Captain J. D. Pratt, Union Provost Marshall in Harpers Ferry, West Virginia. The text of the letter follows:

Colonel,

I have the honor to forward to you under guard two (2) female prisoners, bogus soldiers entitled Kate alias James Johnson and Eliza Frances alias Frank Glen. They were arrested for loitering about the camps dressed in the

U.S. uniform and claiming to belong to Company "K" 1st West Virginia Calvary. It is reported that they have another companion, if not several, of the same "persuasion" who will be "gobbled" up as speedily as possible by military authorities. I would respectfully recommend that you make a levy on some of the generous feminines of Baltimore for a proper suit of wearing apparel for the benefit of these wayward damsels.

A woman's place is **anywhere** she wants it to be! Agree?

When & Why
AND
This & That

"So, Those Were the Good Old Days?"

Recently, I was rummaging through some boxes containing old newspapers and magazine clippings, pamphlets, postcards, and other memorabilia, most of them dating back more than 60 years. Among the "finds" I unearthed is a scrapbook dated "1932" with the hand-printed title on its cover "Laff Notes". It consists mostly of clippings from the little newspaper "The Pathfinder", which as I recall was a weekly news publication that was passed out in my high school civics class. Incidentally, 1932 was the year I graduated from Armstrong High School in Richmond, Virginia, so little clippings were gathered and pasted in the scrapbook that year. I thought it might be interesting and entertaining for you if I shared some of them with you. Remember, in 1932, this nation was in the throes of a deep economic depression that not only swept throughout this entire nation, but the entire western world as well.

Here are some of the "little gems":

- Men's suits made in Poland are being sold in London at $3.10 each with extra pants at $.85 a pair.
- A new Florida law makes barbers professional men, placing them in the same class with doctors.
- A tourist hotel in the Bavarian Alps requires tourists to pay in full before climbing the mountains.
- A big New York nite club can expect about $30,000.00 worth of rubber checks a season.
- The University of Chicago has a fountain pen filling station where a pen may be filled for a penny,

(before the ball point pen was developed).

- Unemployed drifters making for California's balmy climate are stopped at the border and put to work shoveling snow.

- Chicago gangsters were carrying their birth certificates to show police when the police were more interested in seeing their death certificates (this was the Al Capone era of gangsterism).

- Prisoners at Leavenworth Prison were served rabbit for Thanksgiving dinner instead of the usual turkey.

- Just to prove it can be done, W. A. Clark of Baltimore has made a purse from a sow's ear and lined it with silk.

- Judge Emery of Portland, Maine, ruled that a man of 85 is not capable of stealing the love of a woman and directed a not guilty verdict for Abram Milken, that age, who had been sued for $25,000 heart balm by George Felch, 79, who charged Milken had won the affection of his wife.

- And now, my final 1932 "words of wisdom" item. It isn't a woman getting the last word that nettles a man: it's her delay in reaching it. I better quit now in case I want to spend another day with my spouse of 60 years. So long folks.

"What You See IS What You Get - - 1947/1997"

Recently I was reminded of a 1947 story in a Columbus, Ohio newspaper. In 1947, my family and I resided in Columbus and it was the year I purchased the "first-on-the-block" television set. It had a 7-inch picture tube and my family of five, often joined by several neighbors, sat in folding chairs in front of the set in a tight semi-circle. In those days we looked at anything that was on the screen of our "little miracle."

The newspaper article I refer to was an account of a man and his treatment of his newly-acquired TV. It said that he was so upset at what he was then viewing that he got out his shotgun and blasted the thing to smithereens! What triggered my recall of the 1947 newspaper story was a one-time survey I conducted of the six o'clock evening news on one of Washington, DC's most popular TV stations. What I set about to do was count the number of negative vs. the number of positive news items that would be reported. Of course I had a good idea as to what the results of my survey would be before I turned on the TV. And I knew I would be upset, but, hopefully, not so upset that I would, like the guy in 1947, murder my precious 19-inch screen Sony!

And now, the results of the survey of the first half hour of news, consisting of 14 individual items:

Rape 3
Child abduction 1
Attempted child abduction 2
Murder 2
Auto accident death 1
City of Washington,
DC financial and
personnel problems 3

The one positive item in my survey was a report on the great outpouring of financial and other help to a tornado-stricken community. So the results of my little "research project" were 14 for the **negative** side and one (1) for the positive side. In baseball parlance that would be considered a rout of the positive team!

What can we do (or want to do) about the apparent fascination by the public with the outpouring of stories on violence, sexual aberrations, death, and destruction? The immediate answer is probably "not very much" because both the print and electronic media know what the public wants. And, by golly, that is what it is going to get in bigger and bigger portions! Now, tell me, what has happened to the "good old public-indignation approach" to getting a job done? Would not it be worth demonstrating our outrage for the sake of our young people's physical, mental, and spiritual well-being? We and they are being fed unbalanced media meals of sex soup, kidnap salads, and a variety of murder entrees. Think that over, will you? So much for the news.

"Friendship and Some 'What If's'"

I had been undergoing a series of tests as a part of my annual physical examination. For these tests, my primary physician had referred me to a number of specialists who thoroughly checked me out "from head to toe." There were several tests that indicated I needed some remedial attention, and at 84 1/2 years old, it had caused me to ruminate on a few "what if's" ---"what if this or what if that" were a serious health problem.

A number of my close friends know about my health concerns, and one or more of them was in daily telephone contact with me inquiring as to the status of my health. This caused me to reflect more and more on just how precious friendship is, and what a treasure it is for one to have persons who are sincerely concerned about one's well-being. This thought inspired me to share with you some excerpts from my favorite essay on the subject of "Friendship". It was written by Alexander Smith (1830-1867).

"If a man glances critically through the circle of his intimate friends, he is obliged to confess that they are far from perfect. If pushed hard, he will be constrained to admit that he has known each and all to get angry with sufficient occasion, make at times the foolishest remarks, and act as if personal comfort were the highest thing in their estimation. Yet, thus driven to the wall, forced to make such unforgettable confessions, our supposed man does not like his friends one whit less; nay, more, he is aware that if they were very superior and faultless persons he would not be conscious of so much kindly feeling towards them. The tide of friendship does not rise on the bank of perfection. Amiable weakness and shortcomings are the food of love. My friends are not perfect - no more than I - and so we suit each other admirably. Their weaknesses keep mine in countenance, and so save me from humiliation and shame. We give and take, bear and forbear; the stupidity they utter today salves the recollection of the stupidity I uttered yesterday; in their want of it I see my own, and so feel satisfied and kindly disposed. It is the charitable dispensations of Providence that perfection is not essential of friendship."

To that I say "Amen".

"Hold on to the Good Ones"

Many years ago, I was president of a local interfaith council in the state of Michigan. The council had a weekly 15-minute radio program in which a clergyman usually delivered a short religious message. However, from time to time, a layman, such as myself, presented the message, often on a secular subject. Whenever I presented a message I always emphasized the joyful aspects of one's religious faith, not the "doom and gloom" that some of the clergy presented. There was one message I delivered (repeated several times in several different communities, including Washington, D.C. and Winchester, Virginia) that compared the religious attitude of some people to a football game that had been played between the University of Michigan and the University of Minnesota.

The game was played in the Minnesota Stadium before 70,000 fans. The crowd was in a frenzy of excitement. Michigan led in the last few minutes by 3 to 0. Minnesota had a last chance to score. A pass was thrown by the Minnesota quarterback. The whole stadium rose with thrilled Oh's and Ah's. The ball sailed through the air with deadly accuracy and dropped into the fingers of eagerly awaiting hands. But a tragedy occurred. The ball slipped through the fingers and fell to the ground. Many of the 70,000 people groaned and sank back into their seats.

The one who told me that story used it like this: "So often VALUES AND BLESS-INGS slip through our consciousness without a score." But there is a kind of pass that we never fail to catch, that is the pass that is thrown anywhere in our vicinity in the form of criticism, disagreement, pain or problem. To many of us the air seems to be filled with difficult footballs. They come and they are not meant for us, but we make brilliant catches. We hug pain and trouble and misfortune and every painful memory. There is no dropping them. We are down field for a touchdown. It is strange, is it not, to catch ONLY the troubles and let the blessings and values go?

QUESTION: WHAT KIND OF CATCHES ARE YOU MAKING IN THE GAME OF LIFE?

"Are You Listening?"

For more than 20 years I was a zealous "Ham", which is the term used to identify those of us, male and female, young and old, who have a hobby of amateur radio. My active "Ham days" were in the 1950's and 1960's, ending in the mid 1970's with the theft of my transceiver and other radio gear from my home in Millwood, Virginia.

After passing an advanced FCC examination in 1952, I moved up from radio transmission using the Morse telegraphic code (long and short sounds for letters of the alphabet) to voice transmission using a microphone. And, boy oh boy, what a thrill it was for me to warm up the transceiver and announce: "Calling CQ, Calling CQ. This is K8YZV, Lansing, Michigan, Calling CQ!" There usually followed answers to my call, often several, and sometimes, depending on the radio frequency I was on, from outside the USA.

Now, you ask, "Bill Layton, why a piece in year 2000 on your ancient 'Ham days?'". Well, dear friends, it is to tell you about a very important lesson I had to learn. That being, *"when the other person is talking, it is my turn to listen."* At first I was so eager to transmit MY voice (I believe it is called conceit) that often I did not pay sufficient attention to what my contact person was saying and, as a result, my response to him or her was not satisfactory. Some years later after moving to Washington, DC, and conducting workshops on *"Effective Communication Skills"* (over 150 for the Federal Reserve System and other Federal agencies), I always distributed a printed hand-out containing the following points:

Active Listening Tips

1. Stop Talking! You cannot listen

if you are talking. You must want to listen.

2. **Become mentally and physically prepared to listen.** Clear your mind and focus full attention on the speaker.

3. **Watch your verbal and non-verbal cues.** Pay attention to your body language and facial expressions.

4. **Eliminate distractions.** Don't allow interruptions and noises to interfere.

5. **Think of the person as an extremely important human being.** Pretend you are listening to Socrates. Help the speaker feel at ease. Show a genuine interest in what he or she has to say.

6. **Have empathy for the speaker.** Communicate to the speaker that you understand it may be difficult for him/her to express what he/she is feeling.

7. **Try to determine the objective of the speaker and listen for the primary ideas, concepts, and principles.** Don't prejudge what he/she meant just because you know who he/she is. And don't assume that you know where the speaker is going.

8. **Be patient!** Allow plenty of time and do not interrupt the speaker. Also, remember that if you get angry, you lose perspective and self-control.

9. **Ask questions when appropriate**. Don't bombard, but make sure you are hearing and understanding what the speaker is saying. Try to listen for hidden messages.

10. **Clarify and summarize statements.** This helps a speaker to know that you are trying to understand.

"Pride Goeth Before a Fall"

Yes, pride definitely goes before a fall, but what comes after a fall (physical fall) can be worse -- far worse! Let me explain: On my way upstairs to my bedroom at about 10:30 p.m. on the night of August 20, 2000, my left leg collapsed as I placed my foot on the fifth step up. A month earlier, doctors had discovered four blood clots in that leg. The motion of the leg collapsing propelled me over the banister and on to the floor of the foyer (about a nine-foot drop). My wife, Phoebe, called 911 and within 20 minutes, the Enders Rescue Squad from Berryville, Virginia had me on my way to the Winchester Memorial Hospital. After 12 hours in the emergency room and dozens of x-rays, the answer was "many bruises, but amazingly, no broken bones." Just imagine, an 85-year-old guy performing an act, the likes of which are usually performed only by experienced gymnasts, and with no broken bones!! The probable explanations -- my Pamunkey Indian bones (one of my maternal great-grandmothers was a full-blooded Pamunkey Indian) and the fact that I completely relaxed on my way down during the fall. Now in my "post-fall period," as I recuperate, I keep before me this little message that is inscribed on a wooden plaque:

"Why Worry"

There are only two things to worry about:

Either you are well or you are sick.

If you are well, then there is nothing to worry about.

But if you are sick, there are only two things to worry about:

Whether you will get well, or whether you will die.

If you get well, there is nothing to worry about.

But if you die, there are only two things to worry about:

Whether you go to heaven or hell.

If you go to heaven, there is nothing to worry about.

And if you go to hell, you'll be so busy shaking hands with old friends, you won't have time to worry.

Author Unknown

"Late, But Not Too Late!"

The last essay in my book LAYTON LOOKS AT LIFE bears the title "Some Last Words." That essay is a commentary on the moral state of our nation and/or the times and contains this statement:

> What I am more concerned about than my life span is what I perceive as a radical decline in our traditional moral value. For what I see on television, hear on the radio, and read in newspapers and magazines points to a nation that is alarmingly unclear as to what it ultimately wants to be and where it wants to go.

As we move into the 21st century I thought I would ruminate a bit on the subject of **Ethics** and **Morality**, hoping it might help us to clarify our thinking on the question of whether we as a nation are moving up or down (backward) on the **Moral Highway**. But before you read further, this caveat: I have not, and will not pass moral judgment on anybody or anything, but, "if the shoe fits…"

How we as individuals behave towards ourselves and towards others is a matter of making choices: whether to be friendly or not; whether to be generous or greedy; whether to tell the truth or lie. These and other concerns about how individuals act towards themselves and others are embraced by the term "Ethics" and its synonym, "Morality."

The philosopher Aristotle defined ethics as "practical wisdom" because it concerns itself with what should or should not be done with regard to actions that are good or bad for the individual as well as society as a whole. In the modern, developed society such as ours, the systems of laws and public justice are closely related to ethics in that they define and enforce specific rights and duties. They attempt to repress and punish deviations from these standards, whether set by custom or by law. The prologue to the United States Constitution says that "insuring domestic tranquility" is an object of government. That statement is morally neutral. Thus, laws pursuant to the Constitution are designed to promote a moral as well as a legal commitment.

Hopefully, the above comments will aid us in deciding what we will and what we will not permit to enter out homes, our lives, and the lives of the members of our families -- the young and old -- via the electronic or the print media, or by any other means. The American "moral threshold" over which smut and pornography pass is getting lower and lower, and at the same time its purveyors are piling higher and higher monetary profits. It is late, but not too late, to "turn the tide." The ball is in our COURT!!!

Groovy Girls™
Sleep Over Club

Pranks a Lot
The GIRLS vs the BOYS

Robin Epstein

Scholastic Inc.

New York Toronto London Auckland Sydney
Mexico City New Delhi Hong Kong Buenos Aires

Read all the books about the Groovy Girls!

To David J,
Think of this as your applause break

Cover illustration by Taia Morley
Interior illustrations by Bill Alger, Yancey Labat, and Steven Lee Stinnett

ISBN 0-439-81432-4

© 2005 Manhattan Group, LLC
All rights reserved. Published by Scholastic Inc.
SCHOLASTIC, LITTLE APPLE, and associated logos are trademarks
and/or registered trademarks of Scholastic Inc.

The Groovy Girls ™ books are produced under license from Manhattan Group, LLC.

12 11 10 9 8 7 6 5 4 3 2 1   5 6 7 8 9 10/0

Printed in the U.S.A.
First Little Apple printing, September 2005

How to Build a Bunny
the Groovy Girls way

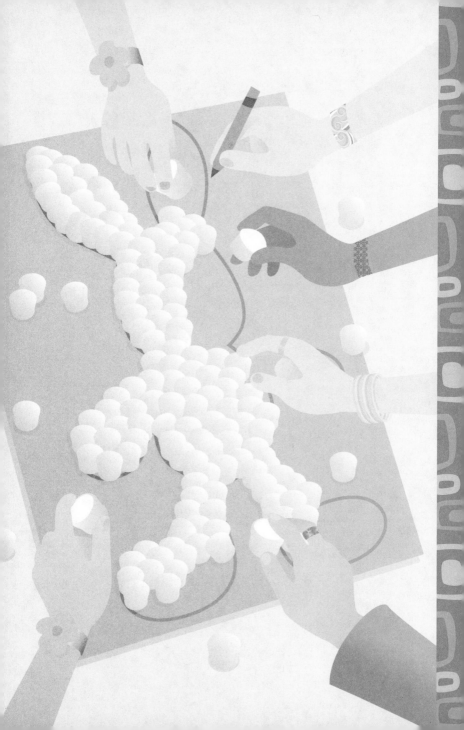

Dear Oki,
The last Groovy Girls sleepover was so supreme, Reese and I want to have another one...
In fact, howze 'bout Sat. night? You free?
Party #2 = 2X the fun!

Chow,
O'Ryan

Dear O'Ryan,
Purr-fect! Love the idea. And I just got glammie new jammies to wear! Can't wait for Groovy Girls Slumber Party No. 2 on Saturday night.
Stay Groovy!

SWAK,
Oki

Dear Oki,

P.S. Wonder if I'll get to see Mike napping on the couch again like I did last time. He looked soooo cute...even if he couldn't stay up all night!

O'Ryan

O'Ryan smiled as she reread her note. She'd written it while Mrs. Pearlman was correcting the class's spelling exam.

Whoever did best on the test would go on to the school-wide spelling bee. So Mrs. P. was concentrating hard as she made big red X's through misspelled words (or "*mispelled*" as Gwen misspelled it).

O'Ryan knew it'd be the perfect time to pass the note.

So she folded the message and nodded at Oki.

Then, she tossed it.

And that's when the unthinkable happened...

Interception!

Mike, the great goalie on O'Ryan's soccer team—and the VERY boy she'd just written about (who thought she was a pretty pizzazzy player herself)—snatched the note from the air.

He grabbed it like a ball heading for the net!

O'Ryan's eyes bugged.

Oki clapped her hand over her mouth.

This was a *deeeeeee-zaster.*

"Spam!" O'Ryan said. If Mike read that note, it would be the most embarrassing—most horrible—most *ugh*-producing moment EVER!

Mike held the note in his right hand and glanced between Oki and O'Ryan. Then he tossed the note up in the air and caught it in his left hand.

He looked at the girls again and smiled.

He hadn't opened the note yet. He just kept tossing it back and forth—teasing them.

Hand to hand. Right to left. Left to right.

I need to get that note back, O'Ryan thought to herself. But from playing on the same soccer team as Mike, she knew he could react fast. She also knew her desk was too far away from his to grab the note back that quickly.

But Oki wasn't worried about desk distance or reaction time. She just wanted that note! After all, it was meant for *her*, not Mike! So when he tossed it in the air again, Oki jumped for it.

Unfortunately, time and distance *did* matter.

And by the time Oki was mid-air, Mike had already recaptured it.

Worse, as Oki leaped up, her chair leg scraped the floor. It made enough noise for their teacher to hear.

Mrs. Pearlman turned around.

The *first* thing she saw was Oki looking guilty.

The *second* thing she saw was O'Ryan staring in disbelief.

And the *third* thing she saw was Mike reading what looked like a little note.

Mike now knew:

1. The girls had caught him sleeping during their first Groovy Girls sleepover on Saturday— *after* they'd made a bet about who could stay awake the latest.

And

2. That O'Ryan thought he looked cute while catnapping.

"Mike," Mrs. Pearlman said. "You weren't just passing a note, were you?"

Hearing Mike's name, Reese turned around. Somehow she *just knew* her twin sister, O'Ryan, was involved in some way.

Gwen thought just the idea of Mike passing notes was funny.

Oki bit her lip and squinched her eyes shut.

But it was O'Ryan's face that told the story.

And told it in bright colors!

Her face had turned as red as a rose.

Mike was silent for a second. Which felt

more like an hour. Then he shook his head. "No, Mrs. P.," he said, "*I* wasn't passing a note. I swear."

Mrs. Pearlman eyed Mike carefully. She wanted to see if her stare would crack him. But Mike stayed solid, sticking to his story.

After all, he *was* telling the truth.

He hadn't *passed* a note.

He'd only *caught* one.

"Well," Mrs. Pearlman replied, "then I suppose no notes were passed." She looked at Oki and O'Ryan again. "Unless anyone *else* would like to clear the air?"

Oki and O'Ryan sat still as stones—they were practically rock candy.

But Mrs. P. was onto them.

"Oki," she said. "Anything I should know?"

Mrs. P. was good at getting answers. But no way was Oki going to fall for her tricks...*this* time.

"Oh, everything's *mar-vy*, Mrs. P. I'm just a little zonked," Oki said, trying to change the subject. "We had a no-sleep sleepover on Saturday night."

"A no-sleep sleepover?" Mrs. Pearlman asked. "What's that?"

"It's where you stay up all night, if you can... but we couldn't," Gwen said, chiming in softly.

But it was just loud enough for Mike to hear.

"Well, if it's *just* that you're tired, take a few deep breaths," Mrs. P. said. "You know, get some air going to the noggin. And then let's continue on with our spelling prep."

As the other students reached into their desks for their spelling books, Oki looked to O'Ryan. She flashed her best friend the thumbs-up sign. And O'Ryan nodded, feeling relieved, too.

Well at *least* they were able to distract Mrs. P.

And Mike *hadn't* turned their note over to the teach.

After all, he could have said, "Nope, I wasn't passing a note. *BUT* O'Ryan and Oki were. And here it is!"

He could have gotten them into BIG trouble.

But he didn't. Chose not to.

Just decided to keep their note private.

Even though he had *read* it.

O'Ryan looked over to Mike, and he smiled.

But Mike's wasn't a smile that totally said, "Glad to help!" or "I'm your new best buddy."

No.

Not quite.

It was more a smile that seemed to spell T-R-O-U-B-L-E.

Chapter 2

Something Old, Something New

"Reese, it looks like you're wearing Grandma's underpants!" O'Ryan said that afternoon after school. Reese had just tried on a pair of long khaki shorts at their mother's store, "Hey, Betty."

"Well, it looks like a rainbow B-U-R-P-E-D on your back!" Reese replied as O'Ryan modeled a tie-dyed T-shirt.

Hey, Betty was a vintage clothing shop. Since being "vintage" meant the clothes were old, whenever the girls were at the store, they got to see all the old-fashioned old fashions.

And they got to go through all the boxes for their mom—which was like a treasure hunt, since you never knew what you'd find. Besides clothes, other old stuff sometimes turned up, too. Like metal lunch boxes with old TV shows pictured on them. And lava lamps, skateboards...even pet rocks!

O'Ryan was especially enjoying being at the store that afternoon because it was taking her mind off some more *recent* history: the Mike note-grabbing-and-reading-interception incident at school that day. In her whole life, O'Ryan had never remembered being so embarrassed, or turning so red!

Helping their mom at the store made the twins feel important, too. Especially when customers asked for their assistance. They'd answer questions like:

"Where are the dressing rooms?"

"Is everything in this bin really $1?"

"Do you think these pants make my backside look big?"

That October day, as the twins went through the boxes, they were also scouting for ideas for Halloween.

If O'Ryan wore the tie-dyed T-shirt she had on, she decided she could be a hippie chick. All she'd need to add were granny glasses and love beads!

Reese hadn't found anything that tickled her yet—except for a hot-pink feather boa. But then, in one of the boxes, she saw something glimmer...

"Hey!" she yelled excitedly. "Check it O-U-T!" Reese pulled a red-sequined beret from the box and put it on her head.

"Looks like you're wearing a mirrored shower-cap," O'Ryan replied.

Reese looked at herself in the mirror and started laughing. That was *exactly* what it looked like.

"When was it in style to wear *that*, Mom?" O'Ryan asked.

"Well, never, really." Mom laughed.

"Too F-U-N-N-Y!" Reese said.

"What's with the spelling, sweetie?"

"It's B-E-E season, Mom," Reese answered.

"We took the test for the school-wide spelling bee today," O'Ryan explained. "I thought it was kind of T-U-F-F."

"That's no shockeroo." Reese smiled, "'Cause that test was T-O-U-G-H. *Not* T-U-F-F."

O'Ryan blew her sister the raspberry, then went back to the boxes. "Funky!" she said, holding up a pair of rainbow-colored socks with spaces for each toe. "It's, like, for someone with monkey feet."

"Hey!" Reese cried, when she got to the bottom of one of the boxes. "I think there's some sort of game down here." She held it up and showed it to her mother.

"That's a Ouija board," Mom replied.

"A *wha-cha* board?" O'Ryan asked.

"It's spelled O-U-I-J-A, but it's pronounced *WEE-jee*," Mom explained. "It was one of my favorite games when I was your age."

"Really?" Reese asked.

"You mean you were actually *our age* once?" O'Ryan said.

"Yeah," Reese said, giggling. "In *vintage* times."

"F-U-N-N-Y!" Mom replied.

"I've never seen a game like this before," O'Ryan said. "First of all, there's no place to put batteries!"

"And second of all," Reese added, "there's no starting point."

"Which brings us to point number three," O'Ryan continued. "There's no finish line, either!"

The board had the letters of the alphabet on it, and the numbers 1, 2, 3, 4, 5, 6, 7, 8, 9, 0. The words "yes," "no," and "good bye" were printed on it, too. And in its box, the girls found a cream-colored, heart-shaped plastic thing-y with a round see-through glass in the middle.

"What is *this*?" O'Ryan asked, pulling out the plastic piece.

"That's the pointer," Mom replied, placing it on the board and sliding it back and forth.

"*Bee-zarr-o!*" Reese exclaimed. "How do you play?"

"Yeah, what's it all about?" O'Ryan asked.

"Well, the game is sort of about telling you your past, present, and future," Mom answered.

"*Whoa.* It tells fortunes?" Reese said, throwing up her hands. "Like it can tell if you guys will ever let me get a dog?"

"That's the idea," Mom replied. "But I might be able to tell you the answer to *that* one just as easily!"

"You're not saying someone knows my *future*, are you?" O'Ryan asked. "Who is this Ouija guy, anyway?"

"This is so supreme!" Reese said excitedly. "I can't wait to ask it what I'm gonna get for my birthday. I wanna play right now!"

O'Ryan, however, got very quiet.

Reese looked at her twin and saw a little twitch in her eye.

She knew that twitch.

It was a twitch that meant Y-I-K-E-S!

"Someone's a fraidy-cat!" Reese teased.

"Am not," O'Ryan replied, turning away.

O'Ryan wasn't going to admit being frightened

of anything—even of a Ouija dude that might know her future.

Even if maybe she *was*.

A little.

"Anyway, at least *this* someone isn't scared of harmless little bugs like someone *else* someone knows!" O'Ryan added quickly.

Reese couldn't deny that bugs freaked her out.

Because *yuck*!

They totally did!

"Well, sure," Reese replied, "but it's completely normal to be bugged by bugs 'cause they're creepy. They're crawly. *And* they're gross. But being jumpy about a board game is just *ba-nanas*!"

"I'm telling you, I'm not scared of some silly, dumb, crazy-lazy board game. That's totally *ree-dic*!" O'Ryan insisted. "And to prove it, I think we should play the game at our sleepover on Saturday night."

"Great," Reese said.

"Great," O'Ryan replied.

So *that* was *that*!

O'Ryan felt pretty proud of herself for *squashing* the fraidy-factor on that one. Plus, with the other Groovy Girls by her side, she was sure she wasn't going to let anything *bug* her!

Gather 'Round, Girls!

"Okay, first thing you want to do," Mom said, explaining the directions of the game, "is place the pointer in the center of the board. Then, lightly rest two of your fingers on top."

"Why?" asked Reese.

"Because that'll help the Ouija board feel connected to you," Mom said.

Once Mom and the girls placed the pointer on the center of the Ouija board and each put two fingers on top of it, Mom continued: "Good. Now you can ask the Ouija any questions you want."

"Like what?" Reese asked.

"You can try asking it about the future," Mom replied. "Or about the past. And you'll see, once the question has been put out there, the pointer is going to start moving to give you a response."

"And what will it say?" O'Ryan wondered.

"It might say, 'Yes.' It might say, 'No.' And it might give you a number, if you ask it something mathematical. *Or*, if the Ouija is so moved," Mom said with a smile, "it might even spell out its response. *But*, that's just between the Ouija and Y-O-U!"

Chapter 3

Practice Makes P-E-R-F-E-C-T

"It's not gonna work," Oki said, leaning over the Ouija board at the slumber party on Saturday night. "How can a Ouija man know our beeswax?"

Since discovering the Ouija board, the twins could talk about nothing else. And *that's* how all the Groovies came to be playing it at their sleepover.

They couldn't even wait until Gwen—or, as they called her, the "*Latest* Greatest Gwen"— arrived, late (as usual).

"She can jump in whenever she gets here," Vanessa said. "Let's start!"

"You'll see, Oki," said Reese, taking the pointer out of the box. "The Ouija will start working as soon as we set the mood."

It was already dark outside, and the fireplace in the living room was glowing, so the mood *seemed* pretty set to O'Ryan already. But...

"Make it darker!" Vanessa said, pointing to Yvette. "Shut the lights and show me some spirit!"

Whereas Oki didn't believe in the power of the Ouija board, Vanessa totally did. In fact, it made perfect sense to her that some sort of Ouija dude out there knew the score. As a natural leader herself—captain of her soccer team and future member of the Supreme Court—*this* was something she could relate to.

"I hope it can tell me what I'm going to look like when I grow up!" Reese said excitedly.

"If you're lucky, you'll start looking more like me," O'Ryan replied, smiling at her twin.

"O'Ryan, we already *know* the board doesn't give scary fortunes," Reese said back, with a laugh.

"Let's start by giving it an easy question to warm up," Vanessa said.

The girls leaned in, and each of them pressed two fingers on the pointer.

"Oh, Mr. Ouija!" Yvette said, in a dreamy and dramatic voice. As an aspiring actress, Yvette really liked to get into any role she played. "On this day, ten days before Halloween—

and right in the middle of spelling bee season— can you tell us how many Groovy Girls there are?"

The girls looked down at the pointer.

They pressed their fingers against it more firmly.

And as each girl pressed, something amazing happened!

The pointer started sliding across the board!

It was slightly jerky at first—more like a skid than a slide—but soon enough, the pointer was in motion!!!

"*Huuuuuh*," Yvette uttered, drawing in her breath.

The pointer slid over to the numbers at the

bottom of the board, moving past 1, 2, 3, 4, and 5. And it looked like it would keep sliding right past six.

But as fast as it started moving, it stopped!

"It stopped on six!" Reese said.

"Way to go, Weej!" Vanessa shouted.

"Wait a sec," Oki said, shaking her head. "There are only *five* of us here!"

"But it must *know* there are six of us."

And then right on cue, the doorbell chimed. *Ding dong.*

Reese opened the front door and in tumbled the "Latest Greatest Gwen."

"*There's* number six!" Vanessa replied to Oki.

"I know I'm late," Gwen said. "But the traffic was just awful!"

"What traffic?" O'Ryan asked. "You only live a couple blocks away."

"Yeah, but there was a traffic jam right in front of your house. See, my mom couldn't drive like her regular speedy self 'cause we got stuck behind Jay's mom's car. And she moves in slo-mo, as if no one's in a hurry behind her!"

"Jay from class?" Oki asked.

"Yup," Gwen nodded.

"Where was he going?" Yvette asked.

"Directly across the street!" Gwen replied.

"Jay was going to Mike's house?" O'Ryan asked.

"You betcha. And he was carrying a sleeping bag and pillow, too."

"Aw, isn't that cute?" Vanessa added. "The boys want to have a sleepover just like ours!"

"Wonder what boys do at a pajama party," Yvette said.

"Probably same as us—paint their nails, braid their hair, and give each other facials!" O'Ryan replied, and all the girls laughed.

"Well, no matter how good the cucumber facial, their slumber party won't be nearly as *beautilicious* as ours," said Vanessa.

"And certainly not as *dee-licious*," Gwen said, holding up a shopping bag. "'Cause, look! I brought marshmallows, graham crackers, and two bars of chocolate so we can make s'mores!"

"Yay," Reese replied, hugging her best friend. "I adore s'mores!"

"Me, too—three, four, and five!" Gwen said excitedly. "Should we make 'em now?"

"No, not yet," Vanessa replied. "We were just playing with the Ouija board, and we're going back to it."

"Oh," Gwen said, plopping down next to Reese. "Okay, but soon, right?"

"We'll see," Vanessa answered. "I mean, we all ate dinner before we came, right?"

The girls nodded.

"Well, without dessert, does it really *count* as a meal?" Gwen asked.

"Nice try, Gwen," Vanessa said, "but no cigar. Let's get back to the game."

The girls had just put their fingers back on the plastic pointer when the phone started ringing.

"I'll get it," Reese said, picking up. "Hello?"

"Yes, hello. I'm calling from A-One Telemarketing, and we're doing a survey."

"Maaaaaa!" Reese yelled. "Telephone!"

"Uh, no! Wait!" the caller said.

Suddenly, Reese clued in to the voice. It sounded an awful lot like a voice she knew. So she motioned to her friends to gather around the phone. Then she pointed to the caller ID screen on the receiver and nodded.

WELLSTONE, ANDREW, the phone screen read. Mike's father's name.

That "A-One Telemarketer" lived directly across the street and, not only that, the girls knew he had his best friend with him.

So now the Groovies knew what boys did at sleepovers:

They made phony phone calls to girls!

"I can't believe they're trying to prank us," Oki whispered.

"Well, they can *try* to prank us, but we're not going to let that happen, right, girls?" Vanessa whispered back. "Keep talking, Reese, and don't let on that we know it's Mike. Try to turn the tables on him."

Reese nodded. "Okay, Mr. Marketer. Now about your survey...you wanted to ask me some questions?"

"Ah, yes," Mike-the-Marketer replied. "A-hem, as I was saying." It sounded like he was trying to deepen his voice to sound like a TV announcer. "Have you and your friends ever wished you'd been able to stay up all night, but not been able to do it? If so, I've got just the product for you!"

"Okay," Reese replied. "Whatcha got?"

"It's top secret, so you need to listen very carefully, okay?"

"Uh-huh," Reese said. She motioned for the Groovy Girls to lean in closer so they could all hear better what Mike was going to say.

"You're *really* listening, right?" Mike asked.

"Yes!" Reese answered, and the girls leaned in closer still.

HOOOOOOONNNNNNNNNKKKKKKK!!

The earsplitting sound of an air horn ripped through the phone. The horn was so loud, it practically blasted the girls off their feet!

The next thing the girls heard was Mike and Jay laughing in the background. Then the boys hung up the phone.

Even though the Groovy Girls *knew* they were being pranked—and had fully expected to beat the boys at their own game—they still got punked!

This was unacceptable!

This demanded action!

Good news was, there were six Groovy Girls against two silly boys. So any way you divided it, the girls were three times as smart, three times as sharp, and three times as spunky as the two boys.

And if this was how the boys wanted to play, the Groovy Girls would play right back!

Chapter 4

Some Bunny's Gonna Get It!

"**Y**ou're kidding! Mike sleeps with a stuffed white bunny?" Vanessa asked.

The girls laughed as they tried to imagine it: Mike curled up with a fuzzy, furry toy rabbit!

O'Ryan hadn't previously told the Groovies that she'd seen Mike asleep with a stuffed animal when she had spied on him during their first slumber party.

But now that Mike had blasted them with the air horn, O'Ryan thought she had no choice but to spill his secret.

"This is incredible info," Yvette said. "Very juicy stuff."

"So juicy, it's practically freshly squeezed!" Reese added.

"And extra pulpy!" Gwen said. "But how do we use it so we don't lose it, you know what I mean?"

"Well, my older sister told me sometimes high school football teams steal each other's mascots," Vanessa replied. "So," she said, "maybe we should try to take his *wascally wabbit*!"

"We can't do that!" Oki replied. "That's too mean."

"Yeah, if we took Mike's rabbit, he'd probably be *hopping* mad!" Gwen said with a giggle.

"Well," O'Ryan added, "from being on his soccer team, I know he's kind of proud. So he'd probably be upset if he even *knew* we knew about his stuffed animal."

"Maybe we should just call him and tell him we've seen the bunny and are going to tell the whole class about it," Reese suggested.

"No," Vanessa said. "We need to be more creative than that."

"Yeah, we've got to do something dazzling," Yvette replied. "Something that shows our razzmatazz!"

"Ooh! I have an idea!" Gwen shouted. All the girls turned to her, hoping she had the perfect plan. "Let's make s'mores," she said, holding up her shopping bag and pulling out the marshmallows. "I am sooooo hungry!"

"*Gwen*!" Vanessa replied, rolling her eyes. "First we deal with the Mike situation. *Then* we make s'mores."

"Fine," Gwen said, hugging the bag of marshmallows to her chest, even though she didn't really think it was fine at all.

"Wait, that's it!" Oki cried, staring at the marshmallows. "We can show Mike we know he sleeps with a stuffed animal by making a marshmallow bunny!"

"Um," O'Ryan said, "explain, please!"

"Bunnies are fluffy, and marshmallows are puffy, right?" Oki replied excitedly. "So we make the bunny out of marshmallow puffs. Then we leave it for Mike on his doorstep. When he finds it, he'll be sooooooo embarrassed. It's a *no-brainer*, right?"

"It's supreme!" Gwen replied.

All the Groovy Girls were in total agreement.

One fluffy marshmallowy bunny coming right up!

"Grab some poster board, glue, and markers, girls," Vanessa instructed. "Then, let's bust open that marshmallow bag and let the fluff fly!"

As the most artistic in the group, Oki sketched the outline of a rabbit on the poster board. Then, the girls took turns gluing marshmallows to the drawing. They had just enough puffs to fill in the whole bunny. And Vanessa used the last one to stick on the cottontail.

"We need to add some sort of message to go with it," Yvette said when the picture was finished. "Maybe we could come up with names we think Mike could call his rabbit," O'Ryan suggested. "In case it doesn't have a name already."

"Yeah," Reese said. "Let's come up with a list."

So the girls started to brainstorm.

"I'd call the rabbit 'Ears,'" Reese said.

"How 'bout 'Honey Bunny'?" Vanessa suggested.

"What about '*Bug-zy*'?" O'Ryan replied, smiling slyly at Reese.

"I'll go with that one," Oki said about her BFF's choice.

"I like 'Carrot Cake,'" yelled Gwen. Then she shook her head. "See? I told you. I can't get my mind off dessert!"

"Ooh, I might name it 'Hare-y Potter,'" said Yvette.

If Mike already had a name for his bunny, the girls were sure their ideas were more clever.

So after they decided on the final list, Vanessa handed Reese the marker. "Here," she said. "You have the best handwriting, so write the choices next to the bunny."

When Reese finished writing "Top Five Names for Mike's Pretty Baby Bunny, by the Groovy Girls," the glue had dried on the marshmallows, and the girls were good to go!

Vanessa carried the poster board, and the Groovies followed her across the street to Mike's house. They carefully set the marshmallow bunny down on the welcome mat.

"Okay, ready, ladies?" Vanessa asked. "On the count of three, get ready to run!" She put her finger next to the doorbell. "One... two..." Then she pushed the buzzer and RANG THAT BELL. "Three!"

The Groovy Girls turned and ran back to the McCloud's, dashing behind the big bush in the front yard. And when they peeked out from it, this is what they saw:

Mike and Jay opening the front door and bending down to examine the girls' art project. Even from all the way across the street, they could see how much Mike was admiring their work!

Not.

At.

All!

"I think I can see steam coming out of his ears," Gwen whispered.

"Yeah," Reese said, "I bet he's turning as red as O'Ryan sometimes does!"

"We got him good," Yvette exclaimed, when the boys stomped back inside. "Great work, girls!"

The Groovies shook their right hands in the air, wiggled their butts, and turned around in a circle. This was their Groovy Girl victory dance.

"Now that that's taken care of—" Vanessa started to say.

"S'mores?" Gwen asked.

"No, not yet, Gwen. Let's get back to that Ouija board first."

So the girls went back inside and sat down around the board again.

It was even darker outside now than it was when the girls had first started playing the game. But instead of this making O'Ryan feel more afraid, now—especially after their successful prank—she wasn't going to let anything scare her. In fact, she was feeling very much in control of things!

"Okay," Gwen said. "Let's give it another try. Ouija board, I lost my hair band earlier. Where is it?" she asked.

The girls leaned in, and the pointer started moving.

P-O-C-K-E-T it spelled out.

Good speller!

"Pocket? That can't be right," Gwen said, reaching into the sides of her cargo pants. She turned the pockets inside out. Nothing.

The Ouija appeared to be wrong.

"Check *all* the pockets," Reese suggested.

Gwen reached into the pocket by her knee. "Whoa!" she shouted, pulling out a pink ponytail holder. "Impressive!"

"Are you kidding?" Oki asked. "You lose ponytail holders in your pockets all the time, Gwen. Everyone knows that! This board doesn't know *anything*...and I'll prove it."

"How are you going to do that?" Yvette asked.

"I'll show you," Oki replied. "Okay, Ouija, if you think you're so smart, what's the name of my cat?"

The girls were *spellbound* as they watched the pointer start to move again.

Well, *most* of the girls were spellbound.

O'Ryan was no longer scared of it—or impressed by it, either. Instead, she was simply amused by the fact that she was guiding the pointer—pushing it where she wanted it to go. And she was pretty sure the other girls hadn't figured this out yet.

The pointer first stopped on the letter **M**.

Then it traveled backwards across the board and paused on the letter **E**.

It slid forward and landed on the letter **O**.

And finally, it came to rest on the letter **W**. MEOW?

"Wow, the Ouija board got it W-R-O-N-G," Reese said. "'Cause we all know your cat's name is Nyan, Oki."

Oki didn't say anything…but she didn't seem happy that she'd proven the board wrong.

"Oki," Vanessa asked, "what's the matter?"

"The word *Nyan* means meow in Japanese!" Oki replied softly.

"Holy guacamole!" Gwen said, totally amazed. "So not only does this Ouija board know what it's talking about, it even speaks a foreign language!"

The girls were so stunned by this (everyone except O'Ryan), that, when all of a sudden they heard spooky noises and saw two monsters in the window, their mouths dropped open. GROUP SCREAM:

"AAAAAAAAAHHHHHHHHHHHHHHHH!!!!!!!!!!"

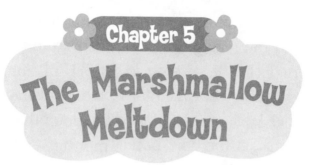

Chapter 5
The Marshmallow Meltdown

"I can't believe they scared us like that!" Vanessa said, fuming as the rest of the girls tried to catch their breath. "And with such a lame prank, too!"

Still, by taking the girls by surprise and shouting "BOO!" Mike and Jay really *had* scared the stuffing out of them.

"Well, maybe the boys didn't see how much they frightened us," Gwen offered.

"Are you kidding?" O'Ryan asked. "You jumped so high, I thought you were going to hit your head on the ceiling."

"Well, you screamed so loud, I thought you were going to break glass," Reese replied to her twin, coming to the defense of her BFF.

"Stop, girls!" Vanessa interrupted. "That doesn't matter now. What *does* matter is figuring out how we're gonna get the boys back!"

Reese and O'Ryan looked at each other. They both knew that Vanessa was right. BUT both also knew that Vanessa was acting like a bossy know-it-all.

And they didn't like it at *all*.

Reese leaned over and whispered into her twin's ear, "Just because she's one grade older doesn't mean she should be so bossy!"

"I'm with you, sister!" O'Ryan nodded.

"So," Vanessa continued, "what are we going to do now?"

The girls thought for a moment.

Which became two minutes.

Which turned into a solid five.

Then they all just shook their heads. They were out of ideas.

"I think my head would *think* better," Gwen said, "if I had something in my stomach."

"You know what?" Vanessa replied. "That's not a bad idea at all, Gwen!"

"Oh, gee, thanks," Gwen replied, rolling her

eyes. Then she turned to Reese and whispered, "Haven't I been saying that all along?"

"We're losing our mojo, girls," Vanessa went on, sounding like a regular General Groovy-nator. "We need to eat something sugary ASAP to bring up our energy. And if we make these s'mores," she added, grabbing Gwen's bag, "it should help us think better."

"I'd say you're thinking better already!" Yvette commented.

The girls ran into the kitchen to get started.

Since Yvette was the one who loved to cook, she started organizing the ingredients. First, she arranged the box of graham crackers and the two big Hershey bars. Then, she reached for the marshmallows.

"Uh-oh," she said.

"Uh-oh-what?" Vanessa asked.

"Uh-oh-we-don't-got-no-marshmallooooowwws," Yvette replied.

"What are you talking about?" Gwen said. "I didn't forget to bring marshmallows. We even used them earlier when we made the...Uh-oh!"

They had used up *every* last marshmallow in the bag to make Mike's bunny.

"Well, you guys must have more marshmallows

around here, right?" Yvette asked Reese and O'Ryan.

"Nope," Reese said. "When Dad went on his diet, he created a 'no marshmallows in the house' rule."

"Did the diet work?" Oki asked.

"Nope," O'Ryan replied. "'Cause it just made him eat the marshmallows faster as he was bringing the shopping bag in from the car to the house!"

"Well, what are we going to do?" Vanessa said, putting her hands on her hips.

"Wait a second," Reese said. "Yvette's a great chef. She might be able to whip up s'mores without marshmallows, right?"

"Well," Yvette said, smiling, "I think even *I* would need at least one more ingredient."

O'Ryan went to the cabinet to see what they could offer as a marshmallow substitute.

"If anyone can make marshmallow-less s'mores work, it's Yvette. She's a culinary G-E-E-N-Y-U-S," Gwen spelled out.

"I think you mean G-E-N-I-U-S," Yvette replied.

"I bet you could even make *this* taste good!" O'Ryan laughed, pulling a jar of pickled artichoke hearts out from the cabinet.

"Artichokes!?" Yvette cried, her face scrunching with disgust. "*B*-to the-*L*-to the *ECK*! BLECK! Those are nasty."

"Oh, come on, Yvette," Oki teased. "You're not giving them a chance. I mean, you're going to have to be more open-minded about your ingredients. 'Specially if you want your very own show on the Food Network someday."

"That's right!" Vanessa nodded. "Think of it as a challenge. You'll be our very own *Iron Chef*!"

"Guys," Yvette replied, "I'm sorry, but I can't make *that* taste good. It's way too yucky. I mean, smell these things!"

When Yvette cracked open the jar, all the other girls leaned in to take a sniff of the stink.

And all their mouths curved into cartoon frowns.

"See?" Yvette said. "Told ya. I mean, if I made s'mores with pickled artichoke hearts, it'd be a joke. A gross joke."

When Yvette said that, a lightbulb went off over Vanessa's head.

"*A gross joke!*" Vanessa repeated. "That's it! Who's thinking what I'm thinking?"

The other girls looked at her blankly.

"It would be a great joke to serve pickled artichoke s'mores to a certain prankster we all know," she continued.

All of a sudden, five more lightbulbs went off over Groovy heads.

"Interesting," Yvette nodded.

"So you want to serve icky s'mores to Mike?" Oki asked, making sure she was understanding correctly.

"To Mike and his fellow joker, Jay," Vanessa replied. "Let's get cooking!"

Yvette took the graham crackers and chocolate, and broke them into squares. She placed the chocolate on the crackers. Then she put them in the pan in the toaster oven.

"This will melt the chocolate a little," Yvette explained.

O'Ryan programmed the toaster, and when the

bell dinged a little while later, the girls carefully removed the pan.

"Mmm," Gwen said, closing her eyes, "you *are* a good cook, Yvette."

"Thanks, but once I add the pickled artichokes, you won't be saying that," Yvette replied.

After she placed an artichoke on top of a chocolate-covered cracker, Yvette placed another graham cracker on top of that, finishing off her creation.

She held the artichoke-stuffed s'more up for inspection. "What do you think, girls?"

"If I didn't know better," O'Ryan said, "I'd eat that in a minute."

"Are you kidding?" Gwen said. "It wouldn't take *me* a whole minute to eat it, if it were a real s'more."

Vanessa looked at the s'more very closely.

She examined it from every angle.

She cocked her head to the side.

She narrowed her eyes.

Then she put her index finger to her mouth, tapping it against her lips.

"I think," Vanessa replied, pausing for effect, "it looks perfect!"

"Yeah," said Gwen, "perfectly revolting!"

"Great job, Yvette!" Oki added.

"Now, let's make a whole plate of these sick snacks and head over to Mike's," Vanessa said.

All the girls pitched in to assemble the fake s'mores. And as soon as they'd laid the last pickled artichoke on the chocolaty graham crackers, they were ready to head back on the bunny trail.

Vanessa was in charge again, with the rest of the girls behind her.

And with their tricked-out treats in hand, the Groovies marched over to Mike's house to serve up their pickled prank!

Chapter 6

Special Delivery

"**Y**ou boys are just better at it than us girls," Vanessa said, handing Mike and Jay the plate of s'mores. "We can't outdo you when it comes to pulling pranks."

"So what are these for?" Mike asked. He eyed the smiling girls and the tray of treats.

"We made them," Oki replied sweetly. "To mark the end of the prank wars."

"Yeah," Vanessa added. "We've come in peace."

"What?" Jay asked.

"Peace," Reese repeated. "P-E-A-C-E."

"I don't get it," Mike said, crossing his arms.

"Here, I'll use it in a sentence," Reese continued. "We hate war, and we want peace."

"*All we are saying, is give peace a chance,*" Yvette sang.

"*Now* do you get it?" Oki asked.

"Not really," Jay said.

"Well, you guys saw how much you scared us when you snuck up on us before, right?" O'Ryan explained.

The boys smiled and nodded at the memory.

"Gwen jumped so high I thought she was going to leapfrog over Reese," Mike replied.

Gwen didn't find this very amusing. "Not funny, Bunny Lover," she said.

"Anyway," Yvette added, "these delicious s'mores are to show you that we give up. You win."

Mike and Jay looked at each other.

Were they buying it?

Or would they see right through the girls' prank?

"Well," Mike said, a smile forming on his lips. "It's about time you girls realized that we're just better at this stuff than you are."

"Yeah," Jay agreed. "'Cause if you didn't give

up, it'd only get worse for you."

"Wow," Oki said, playing along. "We can't even imagine what other great pranks you might have pulled on us!"

"That's right." Mike nodded. "You don't even have a clue!"

"It's good you're doing things you understand better now—like making snacks for us," Jay said smugly, leaning into the tray of s'mores. "*Mmm,* these look good."

When Gwen thought about Mike and Jay taking big bites of the artichoke s'mores, she could feel herself getting giggly. She could sense the laugh coming on. It was like one of those slow-moving sneezes you could feel at the top of your nose!

"Well," Reese replied. "We just hope you enjoy them and think of us while you eat them!"

"Come on, girls," Vanessa said. "Let's let the boys eat...in *peace.*"

"Have a good night, guys!" Reese added happily.

"Good night," Mike said, then closed the door.

It wasn't until the girls got back to the McCloud's that they allowed themselves to look at one another.

Then their full-bellied laughter started raining down in buckets. They laughed harder when they imagined how the boys would look when they ate those icky s'mores.

"Bet Mike would look like this," Gwen said, screwing up her face. She stuck out her tongue and held her stomach.

"Or like this!" Reese said, grabbing at her throat and making gagging noises.

"Or like *this*!" said Yvette, clapping her hands to both sides of her face and bugging out her eyes.

After mimicking the boys, the Groovies ran up to the twins' bedroom and flopped down on their sleeping bags.

In the middle of the sleeping-bag circle, the girls saw a pizza box.

"Thanks for the 'za, Ma," O'Ryan yelled downstairs.

Sure, they'd all eaten dinner, but as Gwen would be the first to say, that was ages ago.

"What should we do now?" Reese asked, grabbing a slice.

"I don't know," Yvette yawned, "but it feels like there are elephants on my eyelids."

"Yeah," Gwen agreed, catching the yawn, and yawning herself. "I'm a little bit tired, too."

And the belly-filling warm pizza wasn't exactly making them want to jump around.

"*I'm* not tired," Oki said. "It's just that my arms, legs, and head are."

"I *know* we swore we'd stay up all night this time," Yvette said. "But I'm not sure I'm going to make it."

It had been a Groovy Goal to stay awake till morning. Since the girls had all accidentally fallen asleep at their last sleepover, they wanted to do better this time.

In fact, they'd made a pact. They'd made a pledge. They'd made a promise.

But their energy was sapping like maple syrup from a tree.

"Okay. I'm making an executive decision," Vanessa said, standing up and putting her hands on her hips.

"I'm calling off the no-sleep part of this sleepover."

"Huh?" Gwen asked, sort of curious. But also sort of too tired to really care.

"If we officially say we're not staying awake all night, we won't have broken our promise if we fall asleep," Vanessa explained. "So on my official say-so, the no-sleep sleepover part of our sleepover is over."

Case closed.

Or so Vanessa thought.

But as Vanessa was making her "official" announcement, O'Ryan and Reese looked at each other. Vanessa was doing EXACTLY the thing they didn't like. She was acting like the boss.

Again!

"Okay,

girls," Vanessa said, as bossy as ever. "Let's get the jammies on, the teeth brushed, and the lights out. Five minutes."

O'Ryan and Reese, with that special twin thing going on between them, suddenly knew what to do. O'Ryan walked over to the stereo and turned it on.

Then she turned it up.

Blast-off-level loud!

Letting the music move her, Reese started to dance. As soon as Gwen saw Reese groovin', she got up to join in. The girls bopped back and forth.

They were poetry in motion!

Vanessa stomped over to the radio and turned it off with a hard flick of the switch.

"Um, excuse me?" Vanessa said. "Didn't we just decide that we were going to sleep now?"

O'Ryan crossed her arms. "No," she said, "WE didn't just decide that."

"YOU decided that," Reese added.

"But we're all tired," Vanessa replied, throwing up her hands.

"That's right," O'Ryan nodded. "But we're also *tired* of you always running the show!"

Vanessa was stunned. "You're kidding, right?"

"Well, honestly?" Oki said. "You *are* kind of bossy."

"Well, I'm sorry you guys think that," Vanessa replied, trying not to sound hurt. "But here's the thing: Taking charge is just what I do. It's who I am, you know?"

"Vanessa," Gwen said, "it's not that we don't want you to be who you are. 'Cause of course we all think you're this great gal—"

"Who's a great leader," Reese added.

"And an awesome soccer player," O'Ryan said.

"But if you think about it," Gwen continued, "everyone here is pretty supreme, too."

"And a lot of us have good ideas and want to have a say in things," Oki added.

Vanessa didn't say anything for a few seconds, but then she nodded. She got it.

"Okay," she finally said. "I promise to try to be more thoughtful about things in the future."

"Thanks," O'Ryan said.

"And I swear I'll listen to whatever you guys have to say—and *then* I'll make the official decision," she joked.

"Hey, I have a great idea!" Yvette said.

"Well, let's hear it!" Gwen shouted.

"Who thinks we should call off the official no-sleep sleepover now and go to bed?"

The girls all laughed, raised their hands, and shouted, "Me! Me! Me! Me!"

And so it was official: The no-sleep part of the sleepover was kaput!

After they took turns brushing their teeth, they washed their faces: Strawberry-scented soap for Reese and Gwen. Pear-smelling scrub for Oki and O'Ryan. Watermelon wash for Yvette and Vanessa.

Then, glammie jammies on, the girls finally got into their sleeping bags.

But before Oki and O'Ryan fell asleep, Oki tapped her best friend.

"Hey," she whispered, "can I tell you a secret?"

"Of course," O'Ryan replied. "What's going on?"

"I'm a little scared," Oki replied.

"You are? About what?" O'Ryan sat up.

"Well, you know how I totally didn't believe in that Ouija dude phantom thingy before?" Oki said.

"Yeah?"

"Well, once it started speaking Japanese, it really freaked me out."

"You mean, 'cause the board knew Nyan's name meant *meow* in English?" O'Ryan asked.

"Uh-huh." Oki nodded.

"Uh-boy," O'Ryan replied. "What's the Japanese word for 'whoops'?"

"Why?"

"'Cause I didn't know you were scared! If I did, I would have reminded you that *you'd told me* what Nyan meant when you first got the cat."

"I told you that? Really? And you remembered?" Oki asked.

"Yeah! He's *your* cat. And *you're my* best friend."

"But still," Oki said, shaking her head, "the pointer moved it to those letters. Not you."

"Sure," O'Ryan replied, "but I was pushing the pointer."

Oki looked at O'Ryan and narrowed her eyes. This sure *did* sound like something her best friend would do.

And Oki also knew O'Ryan would tell her the truth at a moment like this. "Okay, you got me," Oki said, laughing and punching O'Ryan lightly on the arm. "But if you ever try to pull something like that on me again, you are so gonna…" Oki tried to think of a proper punishment. "You are so gonna have to wear my shoes that went out of style last season!"

"No! No! Not that!" O'Ryan laughed. "Anything but that!"

The two girls giggled and lay down in their sleeping bags.

They were totally ready to go to sleep now.

Chapter 7

How Do You Spell G-O-T-C-H-A?

"Ask me how much I love our slumber parties," Reese said to Gwen in Mrs. Pearlman's classroom on Monday morning.

"As much as I do?" Gwen asked, smiling.

"Well, if you love our sleepovers as much as I love my butterfly collection, and the puppy I'm hoping to get for my next birthday, then you totally do," Reese replied.

"I bet Mike and Jay are so not going to want to show up today with the way we got them back with the artichoke s'mores," Gwen said, as she hung up her jacket in her cubby.

"So they're not here?" Reese asked.

"Not yet!" Gwen replied. "Maybe they'll be no-shows 'cause they're sick to their stomachs."

Gwen and Reese laughed, then did a mini version of their Groovy Girls victory dance.

Oki and O'Ryan were also discussing the weekend's adventures. But since Mike hadn't arrived yet, Oki had decided to sit in his seat.

"Look at me, I'm Mike," Oki said, squirming around.

"No wonder you can't sit still. Must be the artichoke s'mores you ate on Saturday night!" O'Ryan replied, laughing.

"Okay," Mrs. P. said as she walked into the room. "Everyone in his or her own seats, please."

Right behind Mrs. P. came Mike and Jay.

Oki batted her eyelashes at Mike when she stood up, playfully holding his chair out for him. "Thought you could use the help," she said, giggling as she returned to her seat.

"Good morning, class!" Mrs. P. said.

"Good morning, Mrs. Pearlman," everyone

responded in unison.

"I hope you all had a good weekend. And I hope that we're all a little better rested this morning."

The Groovy Girls looked at one another and smiled. Better rested?

As *if*!

But was their second Monday of being tired worth it?

In a word:

YesTotallyAbsolutelyOneHundredPercentNoDoubt.

"So we're going to start off this morning with some spelling exercises to help us prepare for the school-wide bee," Mrs. P. said.

Reese leaned over to Gwen. "With all the spelling we did with that Ouija board, I bet we're gonna R-O-C-K the B-E-E!"

"T-O-T-A-L-L-E-E," Gwen replied, misspelling *totally*.

"When I call on you, please come up to the front of the room," Mrs. P. said. "I'll say a word, and you'll spell it. If you get it right, you get a point. Then, I'll ask you to use the word in a sentence, to show you know the word's meaning. If it's a good sentence, you'll get two more points. And whoever has the most points at the end will win a prize."

"Fun!" O'Ryan said.

"Okay, Reese," Mrs. P. called out. "Please step forward."

Reese smiled at her friends as she walked to the front of the room.

"Your word is *pumpkin*."

"Easy," Reese said. "P-U-M-P-K-I-N. And my sentence is, 'I like to carve pumpkins for Halloween.'"

"Very nice, Reese," Mrs. Pearlman replied. "Three points."

Reese high-fived Gwen as she sat back down.

"Okay, Mike, your turn."

Mike didn't make eye contact with any of the girls as he walked to the front of the room. And suddenly, O'Ryan started to feel a little guilty about playing their last prank on him.

She hoped he wasn't feeling too bad about it.

After all, she and Mike had *sort of* been friends before Saturday night's prank wars. The two of them would even shoot hoops in his driveway together sometimes after school.

"Please spell the word *artichoke*," Mrs. P. said to Mike.

"No way!" Gwen giggled.

"Too F-U-N-N-Y," Reese whispered.

But the look on Mike's face was very serious. "Artichoke," he said. "A-R-T-I-C-H-O-K-E."

"Good," Mrs. P. responded. "And now for your sentence."

"Right," Mike said, and that's when the expression on his face began to change.

And as the girls watched him, they thought something seemed strange. It was the way Mike began to smile.

And then it was what Mike said. "I...*LOVE* artichokes. In fact," he continued, "there's nothing I like better than the salty, delicious taste of an artichoke heart."

A-R-T-I-C-H-O-K-E...
I...LOVE artichokes. In fact, there's nothing I like better than the salty, delicious taste of an artichoke heart.

Wait.

What?

Did Mike just say he loved artichokes???

"Okay, thank you, Mike," Mrs. Pearlman replied.

"Well, actually," Mike continued, "I'm not done. Even better than eating artichokes plain is getting to eat them when they're smothered in chocolate and stuck between two graham crackers. That's when they're called artichoke s'mores."

"Mike," Mrs. Pearlman replied, somewhat puzzled. "That's more than enough."

But Mike still wasn't done. He continued.

"You know, if I had to go to a desert island, the one food I'd take with me would be artichoke s'mores. *Mmm, mmm,* good!"

"Yeah," Jay yelled out. "If only I knew where we could get *some more!*"

Gwen looked at Reese.

Reese looked at Oki.

Oki looked at O'Ryan.

O'Ryan looked at Gwen.

(And if Vanessa and Yvette had been in their class, they'd be looking at each other, too. And they'd be looking just as astonished as the others.)

"No way!" Gwen said.

"This is un-*bee*-lievable," Reese replied, shaking her head.

Oki quickly scribbled a note to O'Ryan and tossed it to her.

Dear O'Ryan,

Can it really be true? Do you think the boys really like artichokes? Did our prank go over as flat as a popped balloon?

Yours in stun-dom,

Oki

O'Ryan shook her head. She couldn't believe it, either. Unless the boys were pranking.

And that's when Mike caught O'Ryan's eye as he walked back to his desk. He nodded at her.

And it was a nice nod.

It was a nod from one great prankster
to another.

It was a nod, but more like a wink.

And suddenly O'Ryan got it.

She quickly wrote a note back to Oki,
and tossed it to her.

Dear Oki,

Don't know if the
boys really like
artichokes, OR if this is
just another one of their
pranks. Maybe we're
evenly matched after all.

Either way, can't
wait till our next
sleepover!

Yours in Grooviness,
O'Ryan

MARSHMALLOW MADNESS:
S'mores, Edible Architecture, & More!

Fun Activities
with
BOY BUDS

Throw a Themed
SLEEPOVER
8 GREAT Ideas

Contents

Text by Julia Marsden
Illustrations by Yancey Labat

A Groovy Greeting

HI THERE, GROOVY GIRL!

I t's me, Oki, coming at you with lots of hugs and kisses from all the Groovies! We've been super-busy with our slumberrific fun. You won't believe what happens at our latest sleepover—let's just say there's some very funny *bunny* business going on!

You may be wondering: "Can I throw a supremely groovy sleepover for my friends, just like the Groovy Girls do?"

The answer is: Ab-FAB-solutely!

This handbook is filled with cool and creative party themes—including a Flower Power sleepover (think *Hey, Betty*, O'Ryan and Reese's mom's vintage store) and a Diva Suprema Song Fest bash! You might also be inspired by our book (*Pranks a Lot*) to host a Super-Spirited Sleepover (see pages 8-10). By taking any of our theme ideas and adding your own personal touches, you'll be the hostess of the grooviest pajama party ever!

Wait, there's more! If you love marshmallows, chocolate, and graham crackers—turn to pages 12-13 for some treats that are soooooooo sweet you'll keep asking for s'more! And to keep the marshmallowy thing going, you won't want to miss Edible Architecture (on page 11) and Marshmallow Skyscrapers (on page 14).

So, it looks like you're in for tons of fun! Just remember, whatever sleepover adventure you choose, you'll always be supremely groovy!

SWAK
Oki

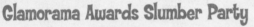

Super-Fun Slumber Parties

C heck out these slumber party themes that include dazzling ideas for dressing up and decorating, as well as great games and activities!

Flower Power Slumber Party

The dress code: *Dress as a "flower child" or "hippie chick."* Set the scene with lava lamps and peace signs. Stage a dance contest using 60s music, and make tie-dyed T-shirts.

Glamorama Awards Slumber Party

The dress code: *Dress as your favorite celebrity.* Decorate with a red carpet and gold stars. Take lots of pictures, sign autograph books, and watch a movie or music videos starring your favorite celebs.

Hula Hoopla Slumber Party

The dress code: *Dress in a tropical print or your favorite beach attire!* Spread out beach towels indoors and treat your guests to tropical smoothies. String leis using paper flowers and learn the hula (see page 6 for more ideas).

Majorly Magical Slumber Party

The dress code: *Dress as a magician.* Decorate with playing cards, black hats, and white (construction paper) rabbits. Then deal out some cards and wow your pals with a few magic tricks.

Groovy Girls Slumber Party

The dress code:
Dress as your favorite Groovy Girl.
Pull a few fun pranks, make s'mores,
and get out a Ouija board!

Diva Suprema Song Fest Slumber Party

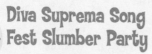

The dress code: *Dress as your favorite musical performer.*
Set the stage with musical notes, stars, and CDs. Then grab a
microphone and take center stage with karaoke, music-video viewing,
a game of Name That Tune, and dancing to your favorite songs.
Does this sleepover sound like it's made for Vanessa?

Really Radical Run-It-in-Reverse Slumber Party

The dress code: *Dress in your favorite outfit worn
backward, or show up in your pajamas!* Hold a backward spelling
bee (E-K-O-H-C-I-T-R-A, anyone?), and play a game of backward
beanbag toss. Serve pancakes for dinner and pizza for breakfast.

Chefs-in-the-Kitchen Slumber Party

The dress code: *Dress in comfortable clothes
topped with an apron!* Invite everyone into the
kitchen and start up an assembly line of food
preparation—like homemade pretzels, make-your-own
pizza, or muffins for the morning! Bon appetit!

Hula Hoopla!

For your next sleepover, why not go Hawaiian? Check out this island-inspired entertainment!

DO create a fun icebreaker. As each guest arrives, take a photo of her "riding the waves" on a surfboard (a folded-up ironing board on a blue blanket or sheet).

DON'T let anyone sit on the sidelines. Have a hula hoop contest to see who can hula hoop the longest.

DO add a touch of the islands to each guest's outfit by making leis. Trim the tops of paper cupcake liners to look like flowers with petals. Plastic drinking straws cut into 1-inch pieces can serve as spacers between the "blooms." Thread onto twine with an embroidery needle. Or, as an alternative, design and use cutout construction-paper flowers.

DO quench your thirst by whipping up tropical smoothies. Here's a fun one-serving recipe: blend a banana, 1/2 cup orange or pineapple juice, and 1 cup of a tropical fruit-flavored yogurt in a blender (with an adult's help), and serve it up. Just for fun, add a fancy straw or a paper umbrella to the glass!

DON'T forget to let your guests create their own fruit kabobs by skewering pineapple chunks, strawberries or raspberries, seedless grapes, and/or peeled banana slices. Use wooden barbecue skewers or colored toothpicks.

DO have fun making seashell magnets. Provide a bunch of shells and craft glue, and glue the shells onto magnets from a craft supply store. Seashell magnets are perfect for hanging up vacation photos, or photos of your friends.

6

Pal Problems—SOLVED!

Whether it's a bossy bud or a bothersome boy, here are some smart solutions!

Know-It-All Friend

Lately, one of my best friends has been acting like she knows everything. She likes to run the show and decide what we're going to do when we get together. What should I do?

It sounds like your friend has something in common with Vanessa—she loves to take center stage! Give your BFF a chance to shine, but let her know that you'd like some time in the limelight, too. Tell her you want to have more of a say when it comes to the things you do together. Just be sure to be nice about it—say that she comes up with great ideas, but you have some good ones, too. Suggest that you take turns deciding on activities, or after each of you proposes an idea, hand her a coin and say, "Let's flip on it." She's likely to get the message without getting her feelings hurt.

Boy, Oh Boy!

The boy who lives across the street is always really nice to me when we're playing basketball one-on-one. But when he's with his friends and I'm with mine, he pretends not to notice me. What's up with that?

So, you're shooting some hoops and sharing cool conversations? Like Mike and O'Ryan, it sounds like you and your neighbor get along great when it's just the two of you. When he's with his boy buds, he may feel pressure to appear uninterested in girls. Don't get caught up in worrying about how he acts when he's with his friends. He obviously likes having you as a bud, so keep the focus on having fun when the two of you are together and he's not so worried about what everyone else thinks. (See page 15 for more on this.)

7

Throw a
SUPER-SPIRITED SLEEPOVER
Have no fear...your guests are in for a Groovy Girls good time!

JUST A LITTLE BIT SCARY SLUMBER PARTY

1. Create some spooky sound effects (see page 9).

2. Give each other manicures using glow-in-the-dark nail polish.

3. Play flashlight tag (see page 10).

4. Have your friends illustrate a scene or picture you describe. The catch? Have them do their drawing in the dark!

5. Freeze dance to ghostly good tunes such as "The Monster Mash," "Thriller," and the theme songs from *Ghostbusters* or *The Addams Family*. (Guests dance to the music, but when it stops, everyone freezes. It's a dance version of Musical Chairs.) Snap photos of guests in their "frozen" poses.

6. Wrap up a mummy (see page 10).

7. Build a spooky story step by step. Have everyone get in a circle in a darkened room. One guest holds a flashlight and begins telling a spooky story. Then she passes the flashlight to the next guest, who continues the story by adding one or two more lines. Pass the flashlight around the circle several times so the story can grow spookier by the minute, if you like. Start with a line like "It was a dark, dark night..." and see how your tale unfolds.

8. Make silhouettes on the wall using a flashlight and your fingers. Your handiwork can include a bunny, an elephant, and a witch with a pointy chin!

9. Pitch "tents" by draping blankets over chairs and positioning your sleeping bags underneath.

8

GREAT GAMES FOR A SUPER-SPIRITED SLUMBER PARTY

Listen up! Ordinary household objects can make for a just-a-little-bit scary good time.

What You Need and Do:
Divide into two groups and have one group hide or turn their backs while they try to guess what sound the other group is creating and what objects are being used to create it.

✳ **Freaky footsteps:** Slowly tap the heels of leather-soled shoes together or against a wooden floor. To create more of a footsteps-on-a-gravel-path kind of effect, fill a shallow box with

dry, uncooked rice. Then stand in the box wearing shoes, and walk in place.

Change the pace of your steps to create the sound of someone taking a slow stroll or making a fast exit!

✳ **Whistling wind:** Fold a piece of waxed paper over a comb,

and use your lips to hum or blow softly against the paper-covered comb's teeth. Or blow across the mouth of an empty glass bottle.

✳ **Roaring thunder:** Grab one side of a sheet of poster board and shake hard to create a roll of thunder.

✳ **Rain:** Pour dry, uncooked rice onto a metal cookie sheet or baking pan for realistic-sounding raindrops. Vary the speed to create the desired type of downpour. Other options? Spray water from the kitchen sink sprayer into a bowl of water, or run shower water into a bucket.

✳ **Rattling chains:** Use your hands to stir up marbles in a metal bowl to create a rattling-chains-in-a-dungeon effect.

✳ **Fire:** Crinkle a piece of waxed paper or an empty potato chip bag to create the sound of a crackling flame.

FLASHLIGHT TAG

Forget traditional tag...shed some
light on a new way to play.

What You Need:
* A flashlight
* A large room, or one floor (several rooms) of the
  house (get the okay from a grown-up first)

What You Do:
* Darken the area where the game of tag will be played.
* Give the player who will be "It" a flashlight, and have
  everyone else hide.
* The "It" guest has to find the other guests by shining
  a flashlight on them. The last person to be found wins
  and becomes the new "It."

MUMMY MADNESS!

You and your friends are sure to wind up having fun!

What You Need:
* Two rolls of white toilet paper

What You Do:
* Divide your guests into two teams.
* Give each team a roll of white
  toilet paper. One person on each
  team will get wrapped up like a
  mummy, using the entire toilet
  paper roll.
* The team that wraps its mummy first wins.

✳ Edible Architecture ✳❀

Sure, you could make a rabbit out of marshmallows for some bunny special, just like the Groovy Girls do. But why not design a house and skyscraper that is good enough to eat?

Home Sweet Home!

Build the graham-cracker cottage of your dreams!

What You Do:

1. Break four graham cracker sheets into halves, so that you end up with eight squares.

What You Need:

💜 Four graham cracker sheets

💜 One cup of smooth peanut butter

💜 One cup of mini marshmallows

💜 Utensils: Butter knife, plate

2. Build the walls and foundation of your house using five graham cracker squares. Spread some peanut butter on the edges of the graham crackers to get them to stick together.

3. After the walls are up, add a ceiling by placing a square on top. Smear more peanut butter on the edges to get the ceiling to stick firmly in place.

4. To make your steepled roof, spread some peanut butter on two opposite edges (the top or bottom, or left and right side) of the two remaining graham cracker squares. Position them on top of the roof, so that they create a triangle.

5. To add to your house, slice some mini marshmallows in half. Dab some peanut butter on one side and "glue" the marshmallows onto the side of your house to create windows, doors, and even shingles.

11

Made-to-Order Munchies

You and your pals can cook up your own customized versions of some popular party snacks by including these recipes on your made-to-order menu! Start with this basic recipe.

Slumber Party S'mores *(Makes 2 s'mores)*

These s'mores are far too delicious to share with the boy(s) next door!

Ingredients:

2 graham cracker sheets

1 flat chocolate bar of your choosing (plain, with almonds, with crispies, or with peanuts)

2 large marshmallows

Utensils: Toaster oven, a serving plate

What You Do:

1. Break the chocolate bar and one of the graham cracker sheets in half. Center one half of the chocolate bar on top of each of the two graham cracker halves.

2. Top each piece of chocolate with a large marshmallow, and with the help of an adult, place in a toaster oven and toast until the marshmallows puff up.

3. Remove from the toaster oven. Break the other graham cracker sheet in half. Then top each toasted marshmallow with one of the two graham cracker halves, and smoosh together. Let stand for about one minute so the chocolate can melt a little, and then dig in!

S'more Brownies *(Makes about 20 brownies)*

Ingredients:

1 (21.5-ounce) box
of brownie mix

5 graham cracker sheets

1 1/2 cups mini marshmallows

3 (1.5-ounce) bars of milk
chocolate, broken into
pieces

Utensils: Large mixing
bowl, medium mixing bowl,
spoon, measuring cups,
13 x 9 x 2-inch baking pan

What You Do:

1. Ask an adult to preheat
the oven to 350 degrees.

2. Prepare the brownie mix according
to the package directions, and spread
in a greased 13 x 9 x 2-inch pan.

3. In a medium bowl, make your
s'more mixture. Break the graham
crackers into 1-inch pieces, and
toss them in the bowl with the
mini marshmallows and pieces of
chocolate. Set aside.

4. After the brownies have baked
for half the time, about 15 minutes,
have an adult remove the pan from
the oven. Sprinkle the s'more mixture
evenly on top. Bake for the rest of
the time the recipe calls for, about
15 minutes. Allow the brownies to
cool before cutting into squares.

S'mores in a Jar *(Makes 1 gift jar)*

What You Do:

Ingredients:

1 sheet of graham crackers
mushed into crumbs

1/3 cup brown sugar

1 1/2 cups mini marshmallows

1 cup milk chocolate chips

Utensils: Measuring cups,
spoon, 1-quart jar with lid,
card stock, scissors, pen,
ribbon, hole punch

1. Layer the ingredients listed in the
box on the left in a 1-quart glass jar.

2. Using card stock and a pen,
create a gift tag that reads:
*Empty contents of the jar into a
bowl. Add 1/2 cup melted butter and
1 teaspoon vanilla extract. Mix well;
then pour into a greased 9 x 9-inch
pan. Bake at 350 degrees for 15 minutes.*

3. Make a hole in the gift tag with
a hole punch and tie the gift tag
around the jar with ribbon.

MARSHMALLOW SKYSCRAPERS

Toothpicks turn marshmallows into a sweet-to-eat tower of fun.

What You Need:

- Mini marshmallows
- Colored wooden toothpicks
- A large piece of cardboard

What You Do:

1. Begin by making the foundation of your tower. Use four toothpicks and four marshmallows to create a marshmallow square (stick the marshmallows onto the ends of the toothpicks to do this). Lay the square flat on your cardboard.

2. Add more squares onto your first square (laying them all flat), until you think you have a sturdy foundation for your skyscraper.

3. Now you can start building by adding vertical and horizontal squares. You can also build your skyscraper with triangles, using three toothpicks and three marshmallows.

4. Will your marshmallow masterpiece touch the clouds or topple to the ground? Keep adding those toothpicks and marshmallows to find out!

5. For some more fluffy fun— have a marshmallow skyscraper contest! Break up into teams and distribute marshmallows and toothpicks to each team. The team that builds the tallest marshmallow skyscraper the fastest wins!

Let's Hear It for the BOYS!

Friends who play together stay together. These sound like words to live by, if you're like the Groovy Girls. But what if some of your friends are boys? No biggie! Here are some great ways to have fun with a boy bud.

Shoot some hoops.

Check out the wildlife (bugs and birds) in your backyard.

Teach each other (and play) computer games.

Make sketches of your favorite animals.

Let him help you come up with birthday gift ideas for your brother (or dad, uncle, or cousin), while you share your gift ideas for his sister or mom.

Create new lyrics for a Top Ten tune.

Practice your soccer moves.

Tell each other lame jokes.

Whip up a really weird snack such as Mud, Dirt, and Worms. (To do this: prepare instant chocolate pudding, stir in some Gummi worms, and sprinkle crushed chocolate cookies on top.)

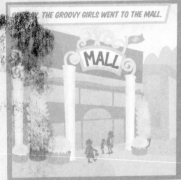